Nick Vandome

Mac Computing for Seniors

For the Over 50s

In easy steps is an imprint of In Easy Steps Limited
Southfield Road · Southam
Warwickshire CV47 0FB · United Kingdom
www.ineasysteps.com

Printed and bound in the United Kingdom

ISBN-13 978-1-84078-335-3
ISBN-10 1-84078-335-4

Contents

1 Introduction   7

Life and times of Apple   8
Choosing a Mac   9
The Mac operating system   10
Ports and slots explained   11
The Mac desktop   12
Customizing your Mac   13
Changing the background   14
Changing the screen saver   15
Changing the screen size   16
Changing the text size   17
Adjusting the volume   18
Customizing the mouse   19
Customizing the keyboard   20
Sharing with Windows   21
Shutting down and sleeping   22

2 Finding your way around   23

Finder: the core of your Mac   24
Quick Look   27
Covers   28
Using the Dock   29
Spaces   34
Exposé   36
Working with open windows   37
Mac programs   38
Installing a program   39
Removing items   40

3   Organizing your Mac   41

Creating files   42
Saving files   43
Opening items   44
Creating a folder structure   45
Compiling an address book   46
Adding a calendar   48
Using reminders   51
Finding things   52
Adding a printer   55
Connecting a camera   56

4   Leisure time   57

Downloading your photos   58
Viewing photos   59
Slideshows   60
Creating a photo album   61
Enhancing your photos   63
Sharing your photos   67
Playing a music CD   68
Organizing your music   69
Downloading music   71
Adding an iPod   73
Earbuds and headphones   74
Creating music   75
Listening to the radio   77
Creating a home movie   78
Sharing a home movie   80
Playing chess   84

5   At home   85

Productivity options   86

Accessing a dictionary 87
Creating a letter 89
Formatting a newsletter 92
Using a calculator 96
Doing household accounts 97
Creating a presentation 100

6 Getting online 103

Accessing the Internet 104
Around the Web 105
Setting a homepage 108
Using tabs 109
Searching the Web 110
Adding bookmarks 111
Viewing your online history 113
Using SnapBack 114

7 Being interactive online 115

Shopping online 116
Booking a vacation 118
Researching family history 120
Price comparison sites 122
Shopping on eBay 124
Using online banking 127
Stocks and shares online 128
Maps online 129
Online games 130

8 Keeping in touch 131

Setting up email 132
Adding mailboxes 133

Creating email   134
Attaching photos   136
Email stationery   138
Dealing with junk email   139
Text and video chatting   140

9 Sharing online   141

Sharing with .Mac   142
Creating an iDisk   144
iDisk preferences   146
Synchronizing with .Mac   147
Sharing photos online   148
Viewing a Web Gallery   151
Creating your own website   152
Sending iCards   156
Creating a group   158

10 Expanding your horizons 159

Adding users   160
Login options   162
Switching between users   164
Parental controls   165
Creating your own network   170
Sharing on a network   173

11 Safety net   177

Mac security   178
Updating software   179
Checking your system   180
Dealing with crashes   183
Backing up   184

Index   187

1 Introduction

Mac computers are renowned for their ease-of-use, stability and security, with good reason. They are an excellent option for anyone, particularly senior users, since they usually do exactly what is required of them. This chapter introduces the range of Macs and shows how you can add your own personalization.

8 Life and times of Apple

9 Choosing a Mac

10 The Mac operating system

11 Ports and slots explained

12 The Mac desktop

13 Customizing your Mac

14 Changing the background

15 Changing the screen saver

16 Changing the screen size

17 Changing the text size

18 Adjusting the volume

19 Customizing the mouse

20 Customizing the keyboard

21 Sharing with Windows

22 Shutting down and sleeping

Life and times of Apple

Apple, the makers of Mac computers, was founded in California in 1976 by Steve Jobs, Steve Wozniak and Ronald Wayne. Originally called Apple Computer the initial emphasis of the company was very much on personal computers. After some innovative early machines, Steve Jobs decided that the next Apple computer had to have a Graphical User Interface (GUI). This is a computer that can be controlled by the user with a device such as a mouse or a joystick. In many ways this was the breakthrough that has shaped the modern face of personal computing.

The first Macintosh computer, using a GUI, was released in 1984. The sales of the first Mac were good, particularly because of its strength using graphics and for desktop publishing. However, shortly afterwards Steve Jobs left Apple which was the beginning of a downturn for the company. Although the introduction of the first PowerBook was a success, the increasing development of Microsoft Windows and IBM-compatible PCs became a real threat to the existence of Apple.

The rise of the iMac

During the 1990s, Apple experienced several commercial setbacks and the company seemed in trouble. However, shortly afterwards Steve Jobs returned to the company and in 1998, the iMac was launched. Apple had always been known for its stylish design but the iMac took this to a new level. With its all-in-one design and bright, translucent colors it transformed the way people thought about personal computers.

The iMac got Apple back on its commercial feet and this was followed in 2001 by the iPod, a portable digital music player. Like the iMac this caught the public's imagination and, since it was not tied to one type of computer, there was a much larger market. Apple have exploited this with dramatic effect and with the addition of products such as iTunes, iPhone and their OS X operating system the future looks very rosy for Apple.

Don't forget

Mac users are usually very devoted to the Apple brand and support it with very enthusiastic fervor.

Choosing a Mac

As with most things in the world of technology there is a wide range of choice when it comes to buying a Mac computer. This includes the top of the range Mac Pro, which is a very powerful desktop computer, to the MacBook Air, which is a laptop that is thin enough to fit into an envelope (if required!). In between these two extremes are a variety of desktops and laptops that can match most people's computing needs. For the senior user some of the best options are:

Desktop

As a good, all-purpose, desktop computer the iMac is hard to beat. This is the machine that helped to turn around Apple's fortunes in the 1990s and it remains one of their most popular computers.

The iMac is a self-contained computer which means the hard drive and the monitor are housed together as a single unit. There are a variety of models that offer different levels of computing power and different monitor sizes. At the time of writing, all models have a DVD writer and come with wireless connectivity for connection to the Internet.

Another desktop option is the Mac Mini, which is a smaller, cheaper, computer that consists of just the hard drive. This means that you have to buy the mouse, keyboard and monitor separately. This is a reasonable option if your computing needs are mainly email, the Internet and word processing. For anything more, the iMac is a better option.

Laptop

More and more people are using laptops these days, as mobile computing takes over from static desktops. In the Mac range, the MacBook is probably the best all-round option. Although not as powerful as the iMac, it has enough computing power for most people's needs. At the time of writing the standard screen size is 13 inches. The MacBook Pro is a more powerful, more expensive, version of the MacBook while the MacBook Air is also more expensive, due to its revolutionary thinness.

Don't forget

All new Macs come with the latest Mac operating system pre-installed. At the time of writing this is OS X (pronounced 10), or 10.5 to be precise, known as Leopard (see next page for details).

Don't forget

If you plan on travelling a lot with a laptop, the MacBook Air may feel a bit too slight due to its very thin design. However, it is surprisingly robust.

9

The Mac operating system

The Mac operating system (the software that is the foundation of how the computer works) is known as OS X (pronounced 10). This is now on version 10.5, which is more commonly known as Leopard.

Apple is renowned for designing operating systems that are easy to use, robust and more secure than their Windows-based PC counterparts. The OS X operating system is based on UNIX, a system that is both secure and has stood the test of time.

OS X is not only easy to use it also has a very attractive graphical interface. This is created by a technology known as Quartz and the interface itself is known as Aqua, which is a set of graphics based on the theme of water.

The OS X interface is immediately eye-catching as soon as any Mac is turned on:

Don't forget

The design of the OS X interface means that some elements, such as menus, allow the background behind them to show through.

Hot tip

To find out more about your current operating system, click on the Apple symbol at the top left of the screen and click on About This Mac.

Ports and slots explained

Every Mac computer has a number of ports and slots for different functions to be performed or additional devices to be attached.

DVD/CD slot
This is the slot into which DVDs or CDs can be inserted to play their content. It can also be used to burn content onto blank DVDs or CDs. This slot is at the side or front of the computer, depending on the type and model of the Mac.

USB ports
These are the ports that are used to connect a variety of external devices such as digital cameras, memory card readers, pen

drives or external hard drives. On most Macs there are a minimum of two USB ports.

Firewire ports
These are similar to USB ports but they are generally used for devices that are required to transfer larger amounts of data. One of the most common uses for Firewire is the transfer of digital video. Firewire ports look similar to USB ones except they are slightly chunkier.

Modem
This is for the connection of a modem cable for a dial-up Internet connection.

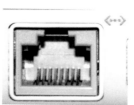

Ethernet
This is for the connection of an Ethernet cable for a cable or broadband Internet connection.

The Mac desktop

The first thing to do with your new Mac is to turn it on. This is done by pressing this button once.

The first thing you will see is the Mac desktop. This is the default layout and, as we will see in the next few pages, this can be customized to your own preferences.

Some of the specific elements of the desktop are:

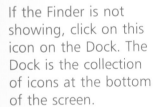

Don't forget

If the Finder is not showing, click on this icon on the Dock. The Dock is the collection of icons at the bottom of the screen.

Apple Menu   Finder Menu bars   Drives

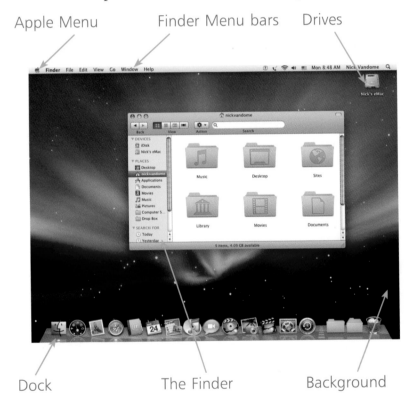

Dock   The Finder   Background

Customizing your Mac

All of us have different ideas about the way we want our computers set up, in terms of layout, colors, size and graphics. Macs allow a great deal of customization so that you can personalize it to genuinely make it feel like your own computer.

The customization features are contained within the System Preferences. To access these:

1 Click here on the Dock (the full workings of the Dock will be covered in detail in Chapter Two)

2 The System Preferences folder contains a variety of functions that can be used to customize your Mac (see following pages for details)

Hot tip

Click on the Show All button at the top of the System Preferences folder to show all of the items in the folder, regardless of which element you are currently using.

Changing the background

Background imagery is an important way to add your own personal touch to your Mac. (This is the graphical element upon which all other items on your computer sit.) There are a range of background options that can be used. To select your own background:

1 Click on this icon in the System Preferences folder

Desktop & Screen Saver

2 Click on the Desktop tab

3 Select a location from where you want to select a background

▼ Apple
 Apple Images
 Nature
 Plants
 Black & White
 Abstract
 Solid Colors
 Pictures Folder

4 Click on one of the available backgrounds

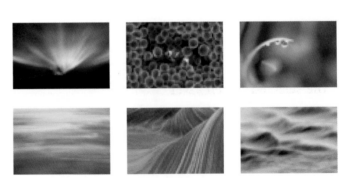

5 The background is applied as the desktop background imagery

Changing the screen saver

A screen saver is the element that appears when the Mac has not been used for a specified period of time. Originally this was designed to avoid screen burn (caused by items being at the same position on the screen for an extended period of time) but now they are largely a graphical element. To select your own screen saver:

1 Click on this icon in the System Preferences folder

Desktop &
Screen Saver

2 Click on the Screen Saver tab **Screen Saver**

3 Select a location from where you want to select a screen saver

Screen Savers

- Computer Name
- Flurry
- iTunes Artwork
- RSS Visualizer
- Shell

4 Click the Test button to preview the selected screen saver

Test

5 Drag this slider to specify the amount of time the Mac is inactive before the screen saver is activated

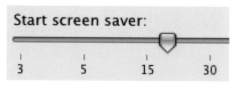

Start screen saver:

3   5   15   30

Changing the screen size

For most computer users the size at which items are displayed on the screen is a crucial issue: if items are too small this can make them hard to read and lead to eye strain; too large and you have to spend a lot of time scrolling around to see everything.

The size of items on the screen is controlled by the screen's resolution i.e. the number of colored dots displayed in an area of the screen. The higher the resolution the smaller the items on the screen, the lower the resolution the larger the items. To change the screen resolution:

Don't forget

A higher resolution makes items appear sharper on the screen, even though they appear physically smaller.

16

1 Click on this icon in the System Preferences folder

Displays

2 Select a resolution setting to change the overall screen resolution

Resolutions:

640 x 480

800 x 600

1024 x 768

1152 x 864

1280 x 960

3 Click here to select the number of colors displayed on the screen (the higher the better)

Colors: | **Millions** |

Changing the text size

Another way to change the size of items on the screen is through the Universal Access options within the System Preferences folder. This is a range of options for users who have difficulties with seeing, hearing or mobility when using the mouse and keyboard. To use the Universal Access options for changing the size of text:

1 Click on this icon in the System Preferences folder

Universal Access

2 Click on the Seeing tab

Seeing

3 Click on the On button to activate the zoom function

Zoom:

⦿ On ◯ Off

4 Press these keys to zoom in on any items on the screen. Use the mouse to move around the zoomed items

Zoom in: ⌥⌘=

5 Click here if you prefer white text on a black background

Display:

◯ **Black on White**

⦿ **White on Black**

Beware

White text on a black background can becoming irritating after a period of time, unless you need to use it for a specific reason.

Adjusting the volume

For users with hearing difficulties there are options for setting the screen to flash if there is an alert sound on the system. To do this:

1 Click on this icon in the System Preferences folder

Universal Access

2 Click on the Hearing tab

Hearing

3 Check on this box to activate the screen to flash whenever there is an alert sound

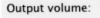 **Flash the screen when an alert sound occurs**

4 Click on this button to test the Flash Screen effect

Test the screen flash: **Flash Screen**

5 Click on this button to access the Sound folder

Adjust Volume...

6 Drag this slider to change the overall volume

Output volume: ◀ ━━━━━━━━━━◯━━━━━ ◀))) ☐ Mute

Don't forget

The volume on a Mac can also be adjusted by clicking on the loud speaker icon that appears at the top of the screen on the Finder toolbar. For more information about the Finder see Chapter Two.

Customizing the mouse

If you have any kinds of mobility problems in your hands it can be difficult to use a mouse (or a laptop trackpad). To use options to make this easier:

1 Click on this icon in the System Preferences folder

Keyboard & Mouse

Don't forget

If you use a Mac laptop, the tab in Step 2 will be for a Trackpad rather than for a mouse.

2 Click on the Mouse/Trackpad tab

3 Drag this slider to change the Tracking Speed (this is the speed at which the cursor moves across the screen)

4 Drag this slider to change the Double-Click Speed (this is the speed at which you have to consecutively click the mouse button, or trackpad, to activate any double-click actions)

Customizing the keyboard

As with the mouse, or trackpad, it is possible to customize a Mac keyboard so that it is easier to use for anyone with mobility problems in their hands. To do this:

1 Click on this icon in the System Preferences folder

Keyboard & Mouse

2 Click on the Keyboard tab

Keyboard

3 Drag this slider to change the Key Repeat Rate (this is the speed a key stroke will repeat if the key is held down)

Hot tip

Click on the Keyboard Shortcuts tab in the Keyboard & Mouse window to access options for keyboard shortcuts for certain functions. The assigned keys can be changed if required.

4 Drag this slider to change the Delay Until Repeat option (this is the time it will take for a key stroke to be repeated if a key is held down. If it is set to Off a key stroke will not be repeated until the key is released and then pressed again)

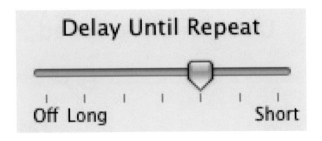

Sharing with Windows

General sharing

One of the historical complaints about Macs is that it is difficult to share files between them and Microsoft Windows computers. While this may have been true with some file types in years gone by, this is an issue that is becoming less and less important. Some of the reasons for this are:

- A number of popular file formats, such as PDFs (Portable Document Format) for documents and JPEGs (Joint Photographic Experts Group) for photos and images, are designed so that they can be used on both Mac and Windows platforms

- A lot of software programs on the Mac have options for saving files into different formats, including ones that are specifically for Windows machines

- Other popular programs, such as Microsoft Office, now have Mac versions and the resulting files can be shared on both formats

Sharing with Boot Camp

For people who find it hard to live without Microsoft Windows, help is at hand even on a Mac. Macs have a program called Boot Camp that can be used to run a version of Windows on a Mac. This is only available with the latest version of the Mac OS X operating system, Leopard. Once it has been accessed, a copy of Windows can then be installed and run. This means that if you have a non-Mac program that you want to use on your Mac, you can do so with Boot Camp.

Boot Camp is set up with the Boot Camp Assistant which is located within the Utilities folder within the Applications folder. Once this is run you can then install either Windows XP or Vista which will run at its native speed. If you need drivers for specific programs these can be obtained from your Leopard installation disc.

Don't forget

Other than for some games, the issue of sharing files between Macs and Windows PCs, and vice versa, have largely disappeared.

Shutting down and sleeping

When you are not using your Mac you will want to either shut it down or put it to sleep. If you shut it down this will close all of your applications and open files. This is the best option if you are not going to be returning to your Mac for a reasonable length of time (say, more than one day).

If you put the Mac to sleep, it will retain your current work session so that you can continue when you wake up the Mac. This option is useful if you know you will be returning to your Mac within a few hours.

The process for shutting down or sleeping a Mac is very similar in both cases:

22

1   Click on this icon on the main Menu bar

2   Click on either Sleep or Shut Down

Sleep

Restart...

Shut Down...

3   If you are shutting down, a window appears asking you to confirm your request

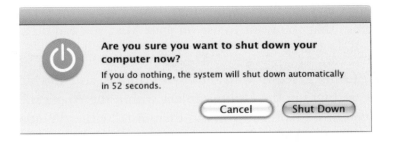

Are you sure you want to shut down your computer now?

If you do nothing, the system will shut down automatically in 52 seconds.

Cancel   Shut Down

4   Click on the Shut Down button   **Shut Down**

2 Finding your way around

This chapter looks at two of the vital elements on the Mac, the Finder and the Dock. It shows how to use these to access and view items. It also shows how to work with different windows and organize your desktop.

24 Finder: the core of your Mac

27 Quick Look

28 Covers

29 Using the Dock

34 Spaces

36 Exposé

37 Working with open windows

38 Mac programs

39 Installing a program

40 Removing items

Finder: the core of your Mac

One of the most basic requirements of any computer is that you can easily and quickly find the applications and documents which you want to use. On Macs, a lot of this work is done through the aptly named Finder. This is the area on your Mac which you can use to store, organize and display files, folders and applications. It is an area that you will return to frequently whenever you are using your Mac. To access the Finder:

1 Click on this icon on the Dock (this is one element of the Dock that cannot be removed)

2 The Finder window has a Sidebar and a main window area

3 The Sidebar can be used to create folders and categories for a variety of items

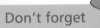

Don't forget

By default a home folder is created in the Finder when you first set up your Mac. This will contain all of your own folders and files. Some of these folders will also be in the Finder Sidebar. These are just shortcuts to these items.

4 The main window displays items within the selected location

Using the Sidebar

The Sidebar is the left-hand panel of the Finder which can be used to access items on your Mac:

1 Click on an item on the Sidebar

2 Its contents are displayed in the main Finder window

> **Don't forget**
>
> When you click on an item in the Sidebar, its contents are shown in the main Finder window to the right.

Adding to the Sidebar

Items that you access most frequently can be added to the Sidebar. To do this:

1 Drag an item from the main Finder window onto the Sidebar

2 The item is added to the Sidebar. You can do this with programs, folders and files

> **Don't forget**
>
> Items can be removed from the Sidebar by dragging them away from it. They then disappear in a satisfying puff of smoke. This does not remove the item from your Mac, just the Finder Sidebar.

...cont'd

Viewing items in the Finder

Items within the Finder can be viewed in a number of different ways:

Hot tip

In Icons view it is possible to view the icons at different sizes. To do this, click on the wheel icon next to the view icon and select Show View Options. Then drag the Icon size slider for the appropriate size.

1   Click on this button to view items as icons

2   Click on this button to view items as a list

3   Click on this button to view items in columns

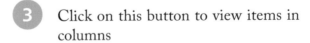

Quick Look

Through a Finder option called Quick Look, it is possible to view the content of a file without having to first open it. To do this:

1 Select a file within the Finder

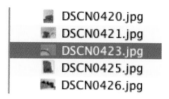

DSCN0420.jpg
DSCN0421.jpg
DSCN0423.jpg
DSCN0425.jpg
DSCN0426.jpg

Hot tip

In Quick Look it is even possible to preview videos or presentations without having to open them in their default program.

2 Press the space bar

3 The contents of the file are displayed without it opening in its default program

4 Click on the cross to close Quick Look

27

Covers

Covers is an innovative feature on the Mac that enables you to view the contents of a folder without having to open the folder. Additionally, each item is displayed as a large icon that enables you to see what a particular item contains, such as images. To use Covers:

1 Select a folder and at the top of the Finder window click on this button

2 The items within the folder are displayed in their cover state

3 Drag with the mouse on each item to view the next one, or click on the slider at the bottom of the window

Using the Dock

The Dock is the collection of icons that, by default, appears along the bottom of the desktop. If you choose, this can stay visible permanently. The Dock is a way to quickly access the programs and folders that you use most frequently. The two main things to remember about the Dock are:

- It is divided into two: programs go on the left of the dividing line; all other items go on the right

- It can be edited in just about any way you choose

Hot tip

Items on the Dock can be activated by clicking on them once, rather than double-clicking.

29

By default the Dock appears at the bottom of the screen.

...cont'd

Customizing the Dock

The Dock can be modified in numerous ways. This can affect both the appearance of the Dock and the way it operates. To set Dock preferences:

1 Select Apple Menu>Dock from the Menu bar

2 Select one of the options for how the Dock is displayed on the screen

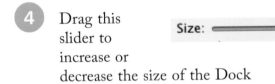

Turn Hiding On ⌥⌘D
Turn Magnification On

Position on Left
✓ Position on Bottom
Position on Right

Dock Preferences...

3 Click on Dock Preferences to access more options for customizing the Dock

Dock Preferences...

4 Drag this slider to increase or decrease the size of the Dock

Size:

5 Check on the Magnification box and drag this slider to specify how much larger an icon becomes when the cursor is passed over it

☑ Magnification:
Min   Max

Adding and removing items

To add items to the Dock:

1 For progams, drag their icon onto the Dock to the left of the dividing line

2 For folders or files, drag their icon onto the Dock to the right of the dividing line

3 To remove items from the Dock, drag them off the Dock and they disappear in a satisfying puff of smoke

Don't forget

Removing items from the Dock does not remove them from your Mac. The items on the Dock are only a reference to the actual locations of the items.

31

Dock menus

Each Dock item has its own contextual menu that has commands relevant to that item. To access these:

1 Click and hold beneath a Dock item

2 The contextual menu is displayed next to the Dock item. Click on a command as required

New Window

Remove from Dock
✓ Open at Login
Show in Finder
Hide
Quit

...cont'd

Stacking items

To save space on the Dock it is possible to add folders to the Dock, from where their contents can be accessed. This is known as Stacks. By default, Stacks for documents and downloaded files are created on the Dock. To use Stacks:

1 Stacked items are placed at the right-hand side of the Dock

Hot tip

To create a new Stack, drag a folder to the right-hand side of the Dock i.e. to the right of the dividing line.

2 Click on a Stack to view its contents

3 Stacks can be viewed as a grid, or

4 As a fan, depending on the number of items it contains

5 Click on an item within a Stack to open it

6 To create a new Stack, drag a folder onto the Dock. Any new items that are added to the folder will also be visible through the Stack

Spaces

Another way for organizing and viewing items on your Mac is the Spaces feature. This enables you to specify certain areas of the screen that will contain specific content items. For instance, you can specify a space for Web content and another one for photo editing programs. To use Spaces:

1 Click on the System Preferences icon on the Dock

2 In the System Preferences folder, click on the Exposé & Spaces icon

Exposé &
Spaces

3 Click on the Spaces tab

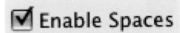

4 Check on the Enable Spaces box

☑ **Enable Spaces**

5 Check on this box to view the Spaces icon in the Finder Menu bar

☑ Show Spaces in menu bar

6 Select the number of rows and columns you want to be displayed by Spaces

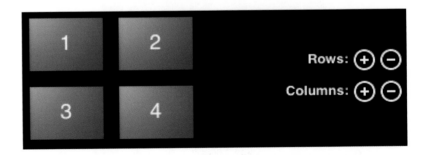

7 In the Application Assignments window, click on the Plus button

8 Select a program to be included in that assigned Space

iPhoto

9 Click on the Add button

10 Select the way in which you want to activate Spaces

11 Click on the assigned activation key to view the items in your Spaces

Don't forget

When you click on an area within Spaces, that content is then displayed full screen.

Exposé

A similar organizational feature to Spaces is known as Exposé. This can quickly let you see what you have open on your desktop, or hide everything from view. To use Exposé:

 1 Click on the System Preferences icon on the Dock

2 In the System Preferences folder, click on the Exposé & Spaces icon

Exposé & Spaces

3 Click on the Exposé tab

4 Select F keys for the operation of Exposé. By default they are F9, F10 and F11

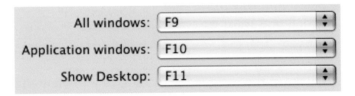

5 Press the keys selected in Step 4 to apply that particular Exposé command

36

Hot tip

Within the Exposé preferences folder it is possible to assign areas of the screen that activate the same functions as the keystrokes. For instance, placing the cursor in the top right-hand corner can have the same effect as using the F9 key.

Working with open windows

When you are working with a lot of open windows it can sometimes be confusing about which is the active window and how you can then quickly switch to other windows.

1 The active window always sits on the top of any other open windows. There can only be one active window at any one time

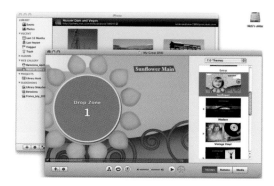

2 Click on any window behind the currently active one, to bring it to the front and make it active

3 At the top left of any active window, click on the red button to close it, the amber button to minimize it and the green button to enlarge it

Don't forget

The three colored buttons are the same on a Mac, regardless of the type of progam being used.

Mac programs

By default, Mac programs are located in the Applications folder. This is located within the Finder. To view and access the available programs:

1 Click on the Applications button in the Finder

2 The currently installed programs are displayed

3 To open a program, double-click on its icon

Installing a program

Although the default programs that come with a new Mac cover a good range of functions, there will almost certainly be times when you will want to install new programs. This could be the Mac version of Microsoft Office or the iLife suite of programs covering areas such as photos and music. To install a new program:

1 Insert the CD or DVD which contains the program

Don't forget

When you install a new program, you usually have to restart your Mac once the installation process has been completed.

39

2 The installation process should start automatically

3 An installation wizard will take you through the process of installing the program

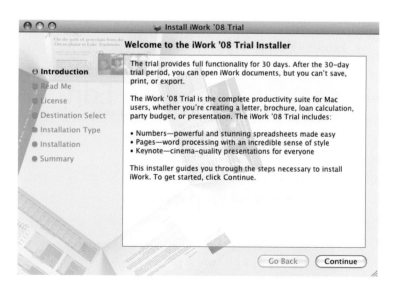

Removing items

As you work on your Mac you will have some files, folders and programs that you definitely want to keep and others that you would like to remove. To do this:

1 In the Finder, click on the item you want to remove

The Great Seal.dvdproj

2 Drag it onto the Trash icon on the Dock

3 To empty all of the items from the Trash, select Finder>Empty Trash from the Finder Menu bar

3 Organizing your Mac

Keeping everything organized on a computer can sometimes be a bit of a headache. This chapter shows you how to work confidently with files and how to organize items on your Mac and add essential peripherals.

42 Creating files

43 Saving files

44 Opening items

45 Creating a folder structure

46 Compiling an address book

48 Adding a calendar

51 Using reminders

52 Finding things

55 Adding a printer

56 Connecting a camera

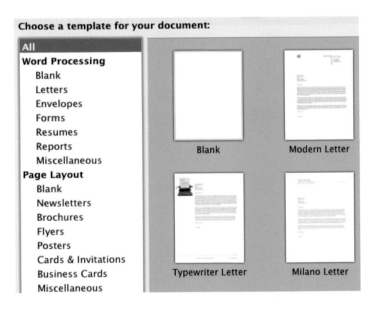

Creating files

There are generally two ways for creating files on a Mac. One is to generate a new file within the program you are using and then save this into a folder. The other is to import files that have already been created, such as digital photographs.

Creating new files

The process for creating new files is essentially the same for all programs:

1 Open the program you want to use

2 Select File>New from the program's Menu bar

3 Depending on the program, there may be a properties window that can be used to define various elements of the file being created

Choose a template for your document:

All

Word Processing
  Blank
  Letters
  Envelopes
  Forms
  Resumes
  Reports
  Miscellaneous
Page Layout
  Blank
  Newsletters
  Brochures
  Flyers
  Posters
  Cards & Invitations
  Business Cards
  Miscellaneous

Blank   Modern Letter

Typewriter Letter   Milano Letter

4 Add the required content to the file

Don't forget

See Chapter Four for more information on working with digital photographs.

Saving files

Once a file has been created it is essential to save it. If it is not saved then it will be lost if the Mac is turned off (although there will be a warning window that will prompt you to save any unsaved files). To save a file:

1 If a file has not been previously saved, select File>Save (or File>Save As) from the program's Menu bar

2 In the Finder, browse to the location where you want the file to be saved

3 If the full Finder window is not showing, click on this button

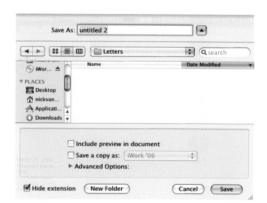

4 Click on the New Folder button if you want to create a new folder for the file

5 Give the file a name and click on the Save button to save the file

Don't forget

It is good practice to save files as soon as they have been created, even before they have any content. Then save them at regular intervals as you are working on them.

43

Opening items

It is possible to open items on your Mac from the Dock or in the Finder.

From the Dock

1 Click on an item once to open it (program) or make it active (file)

In the Finder

1 Browse to the item you want to open

2 Double-click on the required item to open it

Beware

Files can be saved onto the Desktop and opened from there. However, if there are too many items on the Desktop this can increase the time it takes the Mac to boot up and be ready for use after it has been turned on.

Creating a folder structure

As you create more and more files on your Mac it can become harder to find what you are looking for. To try and simplify this, it is a good idea to have a robust folder structure. This gives you a logical path to follow when you are looking for items. To create a folder structure:

1 In the Finder, click on the Documents button

2 In the main Finder window Ctrl+click and select New Folder

3 Enter a name for the new folder

4 Double-click on the new folder to open it

5 Repeat Steps 2, 3 and 4 to create as much of a folder structure as required

Don't forget

Macs use spring-loaded folders. This means that if you drag a file over a folder and hold it there, the folder will automatically open. As long as you keep the mouse button held down, you can do this through as many layers as there are in a folder structure.

Compiling an address book

Having an address book on your Mac is an excellent way to keep track of your family and friends and it can also be used within other applications, such as the Mail program for email. To create an address book:

1 Click on this icon on the Dock, or double-click on it in the Applications folder in the Finder

Address Book

2 Click on an existing contact here

3 Their details are displayed in the right-hand window

4 Click here under the Name panel to add a new contact

5 Enter the person's details

6 Click on the Edit button to finish the entry

Creating a group

1 Click on this button under the Group panel to create a new group entry

2 Give the new group a name

If you update an individual's details, this information is also included in any groups to which they have been added.

3 Drag individual entries into the group (the individual entries are retained too)

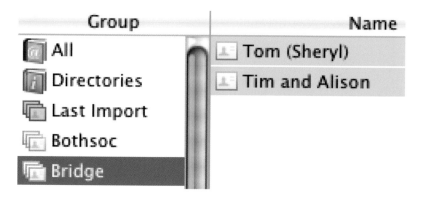

4 Click on a group name to view the members of the group

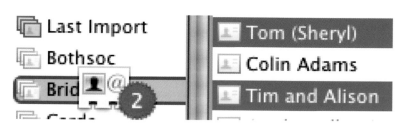

Adding a calendar

Electronic calendars are now a standard part of modern life and on the Mac this function is performed by the iCal program. Not only can this be used on your Mac, it can also be synchronized with other Apple devices such as an iPod or an iPhone. To create a calendar:

Don't forget

Calendar items will be synchronized automatically once you connect an iPod.

1 Click on this icon on the Dock, or double-click on it in the Applications folder in the Finder

2 Click on the Today button to view the current day

Today

3 Select whether to view the calendar by day, week or month

◄ | Day | Week | Month | ►

4 Select a date and Ctrl+click

5 Select New Event

New Event
Paste Event

6 Enter the details for the new event

5
● Party

7 Double-click on an item and select options for how it is displayed

Party
from 08/05/2008 12:00 AM
to 08/05/2008 01:00 AM
Edit | Done

Creating more calendars

It is also possible to create color-coded calendars for different events or activities. To do this:

1 Under the Calendars section, click on this button

2 The new calendar is highlighted as Untitled

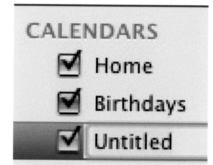

Don't forget

If you check off the boxes next to certain calendars then these entries will not be shown in iCal.

3 Enter a name for the new calendar

4 When you make a new entry, select the appropriate calendar first. Then the entry will take on the calendar's designated color

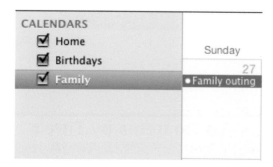

...cont'd

Mini Calendars

There are also options for displaying a mini calendar

1 Click here to show the mini calendar

2 Click on the arrows at the top to move through the months

To Do list

iCal also contains a To Do list, to which you can add reminders for tasks that have to be completed. To do this:

1 Click here to show the To Do list

2 Under the To Do items heading, Ctrl+click and select New To Do

To Do Items by Title ‡

New To Do

3 Enter the required To Do item

Using reminders

Post-it notes are one of the great inventions of the modern world. In recognition of this the Mac has its own electronic version of this invaluable aid. To use this:

1 In the Finder, click on the Applications icon

2 Double-click on the Stickies icon

3 Select File>New Note from the Stickies Menu bar

4 Type the required note

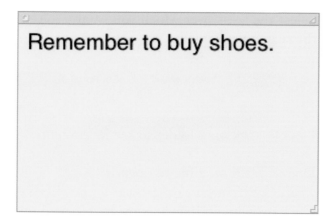

Remember to buy shoes.

5 The Stickie will sit on the desktop until the program is closed

Finding things

Searching electronic data is now a massive industry, with companies such as Google leading the way with online searching. On Macs it is also possible to search your folders and files, using the built-in search facilities. This can be done either through the Finder or with the Spotlight program.

Using Finder

To search for items within the Finder:

Hot tip

When entering search keywords try and be as specific as possible. This will cut down on the number of unwanted results.

1 In the Finder window, enter the search keyword(s) in this box

2 The results are shown in the Finder window

3 Select the areas over which you want the search performed

Don't forget

Both folders and files will be displayed in the Finder as part of the search results.

4 Double-click on a folder to see its contents

5 Double-click on a file to open it

6 Click once on an item to view its file path on your computer (i.e. where it is actually located)

Using Spotlight

Spotlight is the Mac's dedicated search program. It can be used over the files on your Mac. To use Spotlight:

1 Click on this icon at the far right of the Finder Menu bar

2 In the Spotlight box, enter the search keyword(s)

3 The results are displayed according to type

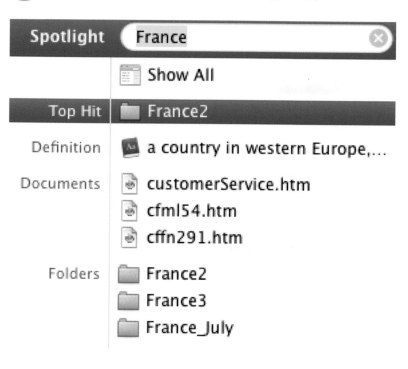

Beware

Spotlight starts searching for items as soon as you start typing a word. So don't worry if some of the first results look inappropriate as these will disappear once you have finished typing the full word.

...cont'd

4 Click on an item to view it or see its contents (in the case of folders)

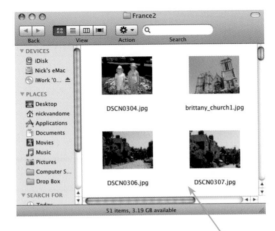

5 If you select a folder, it will be displayed in its location within the Finder

6 Click on the Spotlight Preferences link

Spotlight Preferences...

7 Order the different content types according to how you would like them displayed in the Spotlight search results

Adding a printer

Printers are one of the essential peripheries for any computer and the first step is to install the printer. To do this:

1 In the Finder, click on the Applications icon

2 In the Applications window, double-click on the Utilities folder

3 Double-click on the Printer Setup Utility

Printer Setup Utility

4 In the Printer Setup Utility window click on the Add button

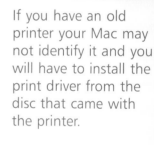

Beware

If you have an old printer your Mac may not identify it and you will have to install the print driver from the disc that came with the printer.

5 If the Mac recognizes the printer, it will install it automatically

55

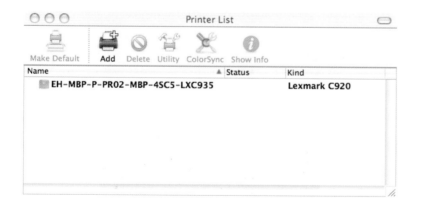

6 If the Mac does not recognize the printer, insert the disc that came with it. This should run automatically and install the drivers that are required for the printer to work

Connecting a camera

Another increasingly essential peripheral is a digital camera. Macs try and make it as easy as possible when it comes to connecting a digital camera and downloading the photographs on it. This is done through the iPhoto program that is part of the iLife suite. To connect a camera:

Don't forget

For more information on iPhoto and working with digital photos see Chapter Four.

1 Attach the camera with the USB cable which should have been supplied with it

2 Attach the other end of the cable to the USB port on the Mac and turn on the camera

3 iPhoto should automatically launch and recognize the type of camera

4 Click on the iPhoto Import button to start downloading photographs from the camera

4 Leisure time

Leisure time, and how we use it, is a significant issue for everyone. For Mac users this is recognized with the iLife suite of software. This chapter looks at how to use the programs within iLife to organize and edit photos, play and download music, create your own music and produce and share home movies. It also covers listening to the radio and playing chess.

58 Downloading your photos

59 Viewing photos

60 Slideshows

61 Creating a photo album

63 Enhancing your photos

67 Sharing your photos

68 Playing a music CD

69 Organizing your music

71 Downloading music

73 Adding an iPod

74 Earbuds and headphones

75 Creating music

77 Listening to the radio

78 Creating a home movie

80 Sharing a home movie

84 Playing chess

Downloading your photos

As noted in Chapter Three, iPhoto can be used to download photographs from a digital camera. If you do not have iPhoto, or do not want to use it, any other image editing program, such as Photoshop Elements, can be used to download digital photographs. But as iPhoto is a dedicated Mac program, this will be used for the following examples.

Once photographs have been downloaded by iPhoto they are displayed within the Library. This is the storage area for all of the photographs that are added to iPhoto.

Don't forget

Once a camera has been connected to your Mac, iPhoto should open automatically. Click on the Import button to download the photos from your camera into the iPhoto Library.

From within iPhoto a variety of tasks can be performed. These include organizing, editing and sharing your photographs.

Don't forget

iPhoto is part of the iLife suite of programs that cover items such as photos, music, web publishing and video.

Viewing photos

There are a variety of ways in which photos can be viewed and displayed in iPhoto.

1 In the main window double-click on an image

2 This displays it at full size (click on it once to return to the main window)

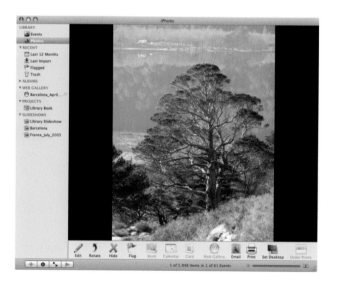

Hot tip

Zooming right in on a photo is an excellent way to view fine detail and see if the photo is properly in focus.

3 In the main window drag this slider to display images in the main iPhoto window at different sizes

Slideshows

A popular way of displaying photos is through a slideshow and iPhoto can be used to produce slick and professional looking shows. To do this:

Hot tip

To select multiple photos, drag around them all, or Ctrl+click on each photo.

Beware

If you only have a small monitor on your Mac a slideshow could be a frustrating experience for all concerned.

1 Select the required images

2 Click on this button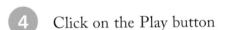

3 Select the required settings for the slideshow

4 Click on the Play button

5 The slideshow will run, with the settings specified in Step 3

Creating a photo album

One of the first things to do in iPhoto is to create different albums (or folders) for your photographs. This is because the number of photographs will expand quickly and it is important to have different locations for different subject matter. This will make it a lot easier to organize your photographs and find the ones you want quickly. To create a new album:

1 Under the Source panel, click on the Add button

2 Enter a name for the new album

3 Click on the Create button

4 The new album is added in the Source panel

...cont'd

5 To add photos to an album, click on the Photos button under the Library heading

6 Select the photos you want to use in the album

7 Drag the photos into the album

8 Click on an album to view its contents in the main iPhoto window

Enhancing your photos

One of the great advantages of digital photos is that they can be edited and enhanced in numerous ways. Although iPhoto is primarily an organizational tool for digital photos, it also serves as a photo editor.

Cropping photos

Cropping involves taking out an area of a photo behind the main subject. To do this:

1 Select a photo

Don't forget

Most photos will benefit from some degree of cropping.

63

2 Click on the Edit button

3 Click on the Crop button

4 Drag the corner resizing handles

5 Click on the Apply button

...cont'd

Color adjustments
To edit the color in a photo:

1 Select a photo

2 Click on the Edit button

3 Click on the Adjust button

4 Drag the sliders to adjust the various color options in the photo

5 The color adjustments are applied to the selected photo as they are made

6 Click on the Adjust button again to hide the Adjust window

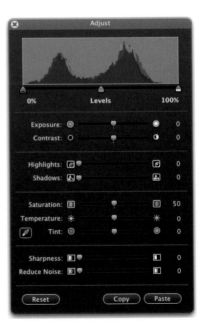

Removing red-eye

Red-eye can be a common problem when using a flash to illuminate photos of people. However, this can be removed within iPhoto:

1 Select a photo affected by red-eye

2 Click on the Edit button

Edit

3 Drag the slider to zoom in on the area affected by red-eye

4 Click on the Red-Eye button

Red-Eye

5 Click on the affected area

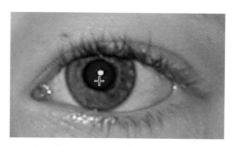

6 The red-eye is removed

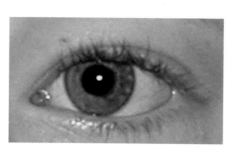

...cont'd

Adding effects

Special effects can be added to photos in iPhoto at the touch of a button. To do this:

1 Select a photo and click on the Edit button

Edit

2 Click on the Effects button

Effects

The sepia effect can create the impression of an old photo.

3 Click on one of the available effects

4 The effect is applied to the selected photo

Sharing your photos

iPhoto offers a number of creative ways in which you can share your photos:

1 Click on this button to share selected photos on an online Web Gallery

Hot tip

For more information about Web Galleries see Chapter Nine.

2 Click on this button to share selected photos creatively in an email

3 Click on this button to print selected photos

4 Click on this button to set a selected photo as your current desktop background image

Don't forget

The Order Prints button will automatically connect you to an online printing service appropriate to your current location.

5 Click on this button to order prints from an online printing service

Playing a music CD

Music is one of the areas that has revived Apple's fortunes in recent years, primarily through the iPod music player and iTunes; and also the iTunes music store, where music can be bought online. iTunes is a versatile program but its basic function is to play a music CD. To do this:

1 Insert the CD in the CD/DVD drive

2 By default, iTunes will open and display this window. Click No if you just want to play the CD

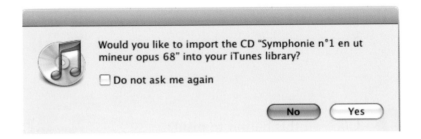

Would you like to import the CD "Symphonie n°1 en ut mineur opus 68" into your iTunes library?

☐ Do not ask me again

No   Yes

3 Click on the CD name

▼ DEVICES

Symphonie n°1 ...

 Beware

Never import music and use it for commercial purposes as this would be a breach of copyright.

4 Click on this button to play the whole CD

5 Click on this button if you want to copy the music from the CD onto your hard drive

Import CD

Organizing your music

iTunes offers great flexibility when it comes to organizing your music.

1 Click here to view all of the music in your iTunes library

2 Click on this button to display a quick view of your iTunes music

Genre	Artist
All (16 Genres)	All (195 Artists)
Alternative	Adoration of the Earth (The Sage)
Alternative & Punk	Agent Blue
Blues	Alicia Keys
Classical	Ana Johnsson
Country	Anastacia
Electronic	Antonio Vivaldi

3 Click on this button to view your iTunes library according to the relevant covers for the music

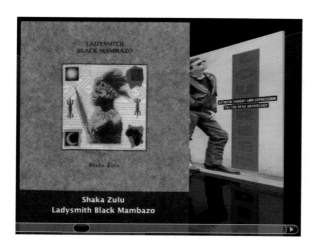

4 Click on this button to play all of the music in your iTunes library in a random order

Adding a playlist

A playlist in iTunes is a selection of music that you want to group together under certain headings, such as for a party or a certain mood or genre. To create a playlist:

1 Click on this button at the bottom of the Library section panel

2 Enter a name for the new playlist

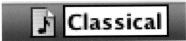

3 Click on the required items of music in the main window

4 Drag the selected items over the playlist folder and release

5 The selected items are included in the playlist

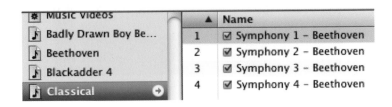

Downloading music

As well as playing music, iTunes can also be used to legally download music, via the iTunes Store. This contains a huge range of music and you have to register on the site once. After this you can download music for use on your Mac and also for downloading onto an iPod. To do this:

1 Under the Library section in iTunes, click on the iTunes Store button

2 The iTunes store offers music, videos, television programs, audiobooks and podcasts for downloading

Beware

Never use illegal music download sites. Apart from the legal factor, they are much more likely to contain viruses and spyware.

71

3 Look for items in the iTunes store either by browsing through the sections of the site, or enter a keyword in the search box at the top of the window

...cont'd

4 Locate an item you want to buy

Don't forget

Once you have registered on iTunes you can then download music to your account from up to five different computers.

5 Click on the Buy button (at this point you will have to register with the iTunes Store, if you have not already done so)

6 Once you have registered, you will have to enter a username and password to complete your purchase

7 Once the item has been downloaded it is available through iTunes on your Mac, under the Purchased button

Adding an iPod

Since their introduction in 2001 iPods have become an inescapable part of modern life. It is impossible to sit on a bus or a train without seeing someone with the ubiquitous white earbuds, humming away to their favorite tunes. iPods are for everyone and they should not be seen as the preserve of the young – although they may select a slightly different type of music to play on them. iPods are designed to work seamlessly with iTunes and the latter can be used to load music onto the former. To do this:

1 Connect your iPod to the Mac with the supplied USB or Firewire cable

2 iTunes will open automatically and display details about the attached iPod

Don't forget

iPods come in a variety of styles, colors and disc capacity.

3 iTunes should automatically start copying music from the iTunes Library onto the iPod.
If not, select the iPod under the Devices heading

4 Select File>Sync from the iTunes Menu bar to synchronize iTunes and your iPod

Earbuds and headphones

When listening to music there will probably be occasions when you will want to use either earbuds or headphones to save other people from hearing your music. The choice between the two could have a significant impact on your overall audio experience and comfort.

Earbuds

These are essentially small plastic buds that fit inside the ear. The most common example are the ones supplied with iPods. While these are small and convenient, they do not usually offer the best sound quality and, perhaps more importantly for some people, they can be uncomfortable to use, particularly for prolonged periods.

Beware

It is worth investing in good quality earbuds or headphones otherwise the escape of sound could annoy people around you.

Headphones

These go over the ears rather than in them and are generally more comfortable as a result. It is worth investing in a good set of headphones because the sound quality will ensure that it is money well spent. The one downside of headphones is that they can be slightly bulky, but some are designed so that they fold away into a small, compact pouch.

Creating music

For those who are as interested in creating music as listening to it, GarageBand can be used for this very purpose. It can take a bit of time and practice to become fully proficient with GarageBand but it is worth perservering with if you are musically inclined. To use GarageBand:

1 Click on this icon on the Dock or double-click on it in the Applications folder

2 Select File>New from the GarageBand Menu Bar

3 Click on the Create New Music Project button

4 Give your new song a name and select any relevant settings. Click on the Create button

5 Click on this button to view available loops of music

6 Click on an instrument type to see the available options

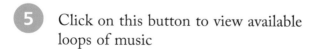

...cont'd

7 Drag a loop here to add it to a song

8 Select a loop and click on the keyboard to create your own music with that instrument

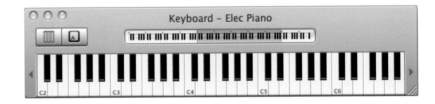

9 Use the mixer to mix each individual track

10 Select File>Save from the Menu bar to save your composition

Listening to the radio

For the radio lover, iTunes offers literally hundreds of digital radio stations. To access these:

1 Under the Library section in iTunes, click on the Radio button

Most major commercial radio stations are not available through the iTunes radio feature.

2 Select a category

3 Select a station from the required category. Double-click on it to access the station

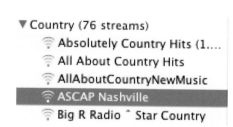

4 The station currently playing is shown at the top of the iTunes window

Creating a home movie

For home movie buffs, iMovie offers options for downloading, editing and publishing your efforts:

1 Click on this button on the Dock

2 Attach a digital video camera to your Mac with a Firewire cable

3 Click here to access the camera

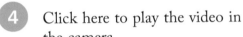

4 Click here to play the video in the camera

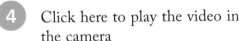

5 Click on the Import button to copy the video into iMovie

Import

6 Click on the Done button to return to the editing environment

Done

7 Downloaded video clips are shown here

8 Drag a clip into the project window to add it to a new video project

Don't forget

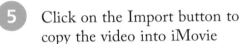

Video clips can be edited by selecting them in the project window and then clicking on the Trim Clip button at the bottom left of the clip. The clip can then be trimmed by dragging the beginning or the end of the clip.

9 Click on this button to access Transition options

10 Click on this button to access Text options

11 Click on this button to access Sound options

12 Text, transitions and sound can be added to a movie by dragging them between the video clips

13 Click Share on the Menu bar and select an option for exporting the finished movie

Sharing a home movie

Once video has been created, it can be shared amongst family and friends on a DVD. This can be done through the iDVD program. To do this:

1 Click on this icon on the Dock

2 Click on the Create a New Project option

3 Give the project a name

4 Click on the Create button

5 Click on the Themes button

6 Double-click on a theme to select it as the background of your DVD

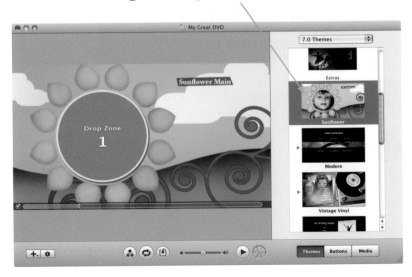

7 Click on the Media button

Media

8 Click on the Photos tab

Photos

9 Select a photo and drag it onto the Drop Zones of the theme

Don't forget

If Drop Zones are left empty a warning will appear when you try and burn the final DVD. However, this can be ignored.

10 Click on the Movie tab

Movies

11 Select a movie and drag it onto the Theme

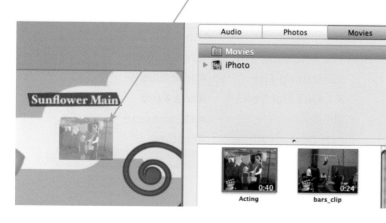

...cont'd

12 Click on the movie name and type a new name if required

13 Click on the Audio tab

Audio

14 Select an audio element that you want to use as background music for the DVD and drag it onto the Theme

Don't forget

All of your photos in iPhoto and music in iTunes are available to include in the DVD, through the audio and photos tabs.

...cont'd

15 Click on this button to edit the Drop Zone

Don't forget

Drop zones can be edited by adding different photos.

16 Click on this button to view the animation of the Theme

17 Click on this button to preview the project

Hot tip

Burn DVDs at a slower speed than the maximum available. This will ensure a better chance of it being burned correctly.

18 Click on this button to burn the finished DVD

Playing chess

Game playing relaxation is not ignored on the Mac and many hours can be spent playing chess against the computer. To do this:

1 In the Finder click on the Applications button

2 Double-click on the Chess icon

3 By default you are white and the computer is black

4 Move your pieces by clicking on them and dragging them to the required square

5 Once you have moved, Black will move automatically

Don't forget

In the Chess application on a Mac it is not possible to play a game against another person.

84

5 At home

This chapter reveals options for getting productive and creative on your Mac, creating letters, household budgets and presentations.

86 Productivity options

87 Accessing a dictionary

89 Creating a letter

92 Formatting a newsletter

96 Using a calculator

97 Doing household accounts

100 Creating a presentation

Productivity options

As well as using Macs for leisure and entertainment activities, they are also ideally suited for more functional purposes such as creating letters and documents, doing household expenses and creating posters or presentations. As always in the world of technology there is more than one option about which program to use when performing these tasks. Some of these include:

iWork

This is an Apple program that is designed specifically for the Mac. It contains a suite of productivity programs including those for word processing, spreadsheets and presentations. Although not as well known as the more ubiquitous Microsoft Office suite of programs, iWork is an easy to use and a powerful option that will fulfil the productivity needs of most users.

Where applicable, the productivity examples in this chapter use iWork.

Microsoft Office

Even in the world of Macs it is impossible to avoid the software giant that is Microsoft. For users of Microsoft Office (the suite of programs containing the likes of Word, Excel, Powerpoint) the good news is that there is a version written specifically for the Mac. This works in the same way as the IBM-compatible PC version and for anyone who has used it before the Mac version will look reassuringly familiar. However, on the downside, Office is relatively expensive and the programs contain a lot of functionality that most users will never need.

TextEdit

For anyone who just wants to do some fairly basic word processing, the built-in Mac program TextEdit is an option. This can be used to create letters and other similar documents. However, it does not have the versatility of either iWork or Microsoft Office.

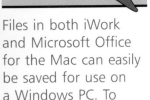

Hot tip

Files in both iWork and Microsoft Office for the Mac can easily be saved for use on a Windows PC. To do this, select the required file format in the Save window.

Accessing a dictionary

A good starting point for any productivity function is a dictionary. On the Mac you do not have to worry about having a large book to hand as there are two options that cover this task.

Applications dictionary

Within the Applications folder there is a fully functioning dictionary. To use this:

1. In Finder, click on the Applications button

2. Double-click on the Dictionary icon

Dictionary

3. Select the option you want to use for looking up a word

4. In the search box, type in the word you want to look up

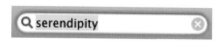

5. The results are displayed in the dictionary window

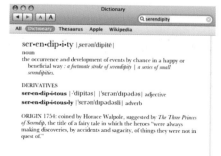

...cont'd

Dashboard dictionary

The Dashboard is a program within Mac OS X that offers a number of widgets, or small programs, for a variety of useful tasks such as weather reports, maps, a clock and a calculator. It also has a dictionary. To use this:

1 Click on this icon on the Dock to access the Dashboard widgets

2 If the Dictionary widget is not showing click on this button to view the available widgets

3 Click on the Dictionary widget to add it to the main Dashboard (which appears above the Desktop)

Dictionary   ESPN   Flight Tracker

4 The Dictionary widget can be used in a similar way to the one on the previous page

Creating a letter

One of the most common word processing tasks is writing a letter and it is something that most of us have to do for either business or pleasure. This could be a letter to a family member or a letter of complaint. Whatever the subject matter it is worth making your letters look as professional, or as stylish, as possible. To create a letter in iWork:

1 In Finder, click on the Applications button

2 Double-click on the iWork folder

iWork '08

3 Double-click on the Pages icon

Pages

Don't forget

There are enough different letter templates in Pages for you not to need to create your own. If required, existing ones can be amended.

4 In the template window, click on the Letters option

Choose a template

All
Word Processing
Blank
Letters

5 Click on a style for the type of letter you want to create

Modern Letter

6 Click on the Choose button

Choose

7 An untitled letter is displayed based on the template you have selected

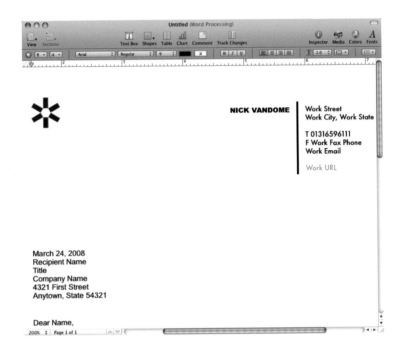

8 Double-click on an element of the letter and overtype to change it

9 Click once in the draft text of the letter. This will highlight all of the text

August 12, 2008
Recipient Name
Title
Company Name
4321 First Street
Anytown, State 54321

Dear Kathy,

Lorem ipsum dolor sit amet, consectetur adipiscing elit, set eiusmod tempor in aliquam. Ut enim ad minim veniam, quis nostrud exerc. Irure dolor in repreher magna aliqua. Ut enim ad minim veniam, quis nostrud exercitation ullamco lat consequat. Duis aute irure dolor in reprehenderit in voluptate velit esse moles incom dereud facilis est er expedit distinct. Nam liber te conscient to factor tur tam. Neque pecun modut est neque nonor et imper ned libidig met, consectet dolore magna aliquam is nostrud exercitation ullam mmodo consequet. Duis a dolore eu fugiat nulla pariatur. ¶

10 Write your own text for the letter

August 12, 2008
Recipient Name
Title
Company Name
4321 First Street
Anytown, State 54321

Dear Kathy,

How are you, it's been a while.

Best wishes,

Nick

11 Select File>Save from the Menu bar

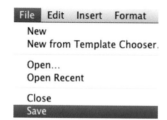

| File | Edit | Insert | Format |

New
New from Template Chooser.

Open...
Open Recent

Close
Save

12 Browse to the folder into which you want to save the letter

Save As: untitled

◄ ► | 88 ≡ Ⅲ | 🗀 Letters

💿 Symphonie n°1 ... ⏏   Name

▼ PLACES
🖥 Desktop
🏠 nickvandome
📁 Applications
📄 Documents

13 Give the letter a name

Save As: kathy_aug_08

14 Click on the Save button

Save

Formatting a newsletter

Newsletters are not just the preserve of the business world: they are a great source of information for local clubs, communities and also for family updates. To create and format a newsletter in iWork:

1 In Finder, click on the Applications button

Applications

2 Double-click on the iWork folder

iWork '08

3 Double-click on the Pages icon

Pages

4 In the template window, click on the Newsletters option

Choose a template
All
Word Processing
  Blank
  Letters
  Envelopes
  Forms
  Resumes
  Reports
  Miscellaneous
Page Layout
  Blank
  Newsletters

5 Click on a style for the type of newsletter you want to create

Family Newsletter

6 Click on the Choose button

Choose

7 Click on a text element to select it

8 Overtype the selection with your own text

9 Click on an image placeholder (this is just a default image that can be changed with your own photos)

93

10 Click on the Media button on the toolbar

Media

...cont'd

11 In the Media window browse to the photo you want to use

The Media browser is a quick way to access your iPhoto Library. However, photos have to have been imported into iPhoto for them to be visible in the Media browser.

12 Drag the selected photo onto the placeholder

13 If required, you can drag the image around the page to re-position it

14 Click on the Pages button on the toolbar to add new pages to the newsletter

15 Click on the type of new page you want to include

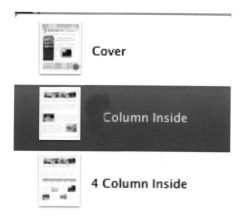

Cover

Column Inside

4 Column Inside

16 Format the new page in the same way as the cover page

Vandome family vacation

Lorem ipsum dolor sit amet, consec tetur adi piscing elit, set eiusmod tempor incidunt et labore et dolore magna aliquam. Ut enim ad minim veniam, quis nostrud exerc. Irure dolor in reprehend incididunt ut labore et dolore magna aliqua. Ut enim ad minim veniam, quis nostrud exercitation aborum Et harumd dereud facilis est er expedit distinct. Nam liber te conscient to factor tum poenullainc ommod quae egen mco laboris nisi ut aliquip ex ea commodo cons equat. Duis aute irure dolor in reprehenderit in voluptate velit esse molestaie aborum Et harumd dereud facilis est.

17 Save the newsletter in the same way as a letter

Using a calculator

Financial matters can sometimes be a chore but they are a necessary part of life, whether it is working out household expenses or calculating available spending money. Even for the best mathematicians a calculator is a trusty friend when it comes to arithmetic. Luckily the Mac has one ready-made:

1 In Finder, click on the Applications button

2 Double-click on the Calculator icon

3 Click on the calculator's buttons to perform calculations

Don't forget

If you are going to be doing anything more than basic calculations, the scientific option may be more useful than the basic one.

4 Select View from the Menu bar and select an option for the type of calculator being displayed

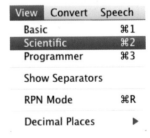

5 The option selected in Step 4 is now available

Doing household accounts

As well as being useful for word processing iWork can also be used for financial accounting, such as keeping track of the household accounts. To do this:

1 In Finder, click on the Applications button

2 Double-click on the iWork icon

3 Double-click on the Numbers icon

Don't forget

Although any type of accounts are a chore, the more they are kept up to date the easier it is to control them.

97

4 In the template window click on the Personal button

5 Select the Budget template

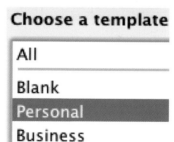

6 Click on the Choose button

...cont'd

7 The budget template is displayed. All of the items can be edited with your own information

Personal Budget

Monthly Net Income

Income Type	Amount
Monthly Net Income	$4,500
Planned Monthly Savings	$300
Available Cash	$4,200

Additional Income

Details	Month	Amount
Mid Year Bonus	June	$2,000
Year End Bonus	December	$3,000
	January	
Total Additional Income		$5,000

Monthly Expenses

Expense	Costs
Mortgage	$2,300
Taxes	$600
Car Payment	$350
Car Insurance	$60
Home Owners Insurance	$127
Cable Bill	$120
Gas/Electric	$88
Monthly Prescription	$50
Total Monthly Expenses	$3,695

Planned Expenses

Expenditure	Month	Amount
November vacation	November	$450
Home for the holidays	December	$600
Gifts for family	December	$300
Family vacation	July	$880
	January	
	January	
	January	
	January	
Total Planned Expenses		$2,230

8 Click on a style to change the formatting of the displayed budget

Styles

Basic

Basic (No Grid)

Gray

Gray Headers

Gray Fill

Beige

9 Click on one of the budget topics

Monthly Expenses

10 The selected element is highlighted

Monthly Expenses

Expense	Costs
Mortgage	$2,300
Taxes	$600
Car Payment	$350
Car Insurance	$60
Home Owners Insurance	$127
Cable Bill	$120
Gas/Electric	$88
Monthly Prescription	$50
Total Monthly Expenses	$3,695

11 Double-click on an individual item to select it

4 Car Payment

12 Overtype the selected item with your own details

4 Motor Home payment

13 Select a cell containing financial information. Edit the information, as required

$120

$88

$50

$3,695

14 Linked cells are updated accordingly

$800

$88

$50

$4,375

Don't forget

Linked cells are controlled by a mathematical equation that ensures that if one is updated then the data in the linked cell changes too.

15 Save the spreadsheet in the same way as for a letter or a newsletter

Creating a presentation

Presentations are a great way to produce customized slideshows of family photographs or promote activities in local clubs or charities. To do this in iWork:

1 In Finder, click on the Applications button

2 Double-click on the iWork icon

Don't forget

Keynote is the iWork equivalent of Microsoft Powerpoint.

3 Double-click on the Keynote icon

4 Click on a type of presentation

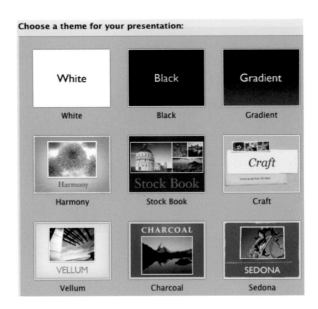

5 Click on the Choose button

6 Double-click on the text to select it

7 Overtype with your own text

8 Click on the Media button on the Menu bar

9 Browse to your photos

> **Beware**
>
> When adding text to a presentation, make sure that it is not too small and that there is not too much of it.

10 Drag a selected photo onto the placeholder photo on the slide. This replaces the placeholder photo (above) with your own (below)

11 To add more text to a slide, click on the Text Box button on the Menu bar

12 Drag the text tool on the slide to create a text box and type the required text

Don't forget

Text boxes can be repositioned by dragging them around once they have been placed on a slide.

13 Click on these buttons for options for formatting the color and *type* of the text

14 To add more slides click on the New button on the Menu bar. Add content in the same way as the original slide

15 Click on the Play button on the Menu bar to preview the presentation

16 Save the presentation in the same way as a letter, a newsletter or a spreadsheet

6 Getting online

Accessing the Internet and World Wide Web (WWW) is essential for most computer users. This chapter shows you how to use your Mac to start browsing the Web.

104   Accessing the Internet

105   Around the Web

108   Setting a homepage

109   Using tabs

110   Searching the Web

111   Adding bookmarks

113   Viewing your online history

114   Using SnapBack

Accessing the Internet

Access to the Internet is an accepted part of the computing world and it is unusual for users not to want to do this. Not only does this provide a gateway to the World Wide Web but also email.

Connecting to the Internet with a Mac is done through the System Preferences. To do this:

1 Click on the System Preferences icon on the Dock

Don't forget

Before you connect to the Internet you have to have an Internet Service Provider (ISP) who will provide you with the relevant method of connection i.e. dial-up, cable or broadband. They will provide you with any login details.

2 Click on the Network icon

Network

3 Check that your method of connecting to the Internet is active i.e. colored green

4 Click on the Assist Me button to access wizards for connecting to the Internet with your preferred method of connection

Assist me...

Around the Web

When you are surfing the Web it is important to feel comfortable with both your browser and also the websites at which you are looking. Most websites are a collection of linked pages that you can move between by clicking on links (also known as hyperlinks) that connect the different pages.

Address bar

The Address bar is the box at the top of the browser that displays the address of the web page that is currently being displayed. Each web page has a unique address so the address changes whenever you move to a different page. The Address bar displays the web page address in this format:

Main content

The full content of a web page is displayed in the main browser window:

Don't forget

Macs have a built-in Web browser known as Safari. This can be accessed from the Dock by clicking on this icon:

105

...cont'd

Toolbar

This is a collection of icons at the top of the browser that has various options for navigating around web pages and accessing options such as newsfeeds and printing pages:

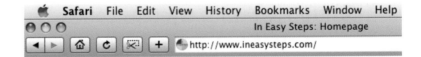

Menu bar

This contains various menus with options for navigating around, and customizing web pages. In Safari it is located at the top of the Safari window:

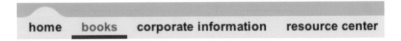

Navigation bars

These are groups of buttons that appear on websites to help users navigate within the site. Generally, the main navigation bars appear in the same place on every page of the site:

Search box

Most websites have a search box, into which keywords or phrases can be entered to search over the whole site:

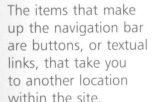

Hot tip

The Toolbar contains a homepage button which takes you to your own homepage i.e. the page that is accessed when you first open up your browser.

Don't forget

The items that make up the navigation bar are buttons, or textual links, that take you to another location within the site.

Links

This is the device that is used to move between pages within a website, or from one website to another. Links can be in a variety of styles, but most frequently they are in the form of buttons, underlined text or a roll-over (i.e. a button or piece of text that changes appearance when the cursor is passed over it):

Don't forget

The cursor usually turns into a pointing hand when it is over a link on a website.

write for us ⋮ accessibility ⋮ feedback ⋮ site map

Tabs

Safari has an option for using different tabs. This enables you to open different web pages within the same browser window. You can then move between the pages by clicking on each tab, at the top of the window:

Bookmarks

Everyone has their favorite web pages that they return to again and again. These can be added to a list in a browser so that they can be accessed quickly when required. There is usually a button at the top of the browser that can add the current page to the list of bookmarked items:

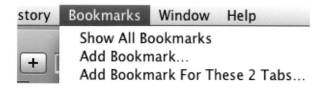

Setting a homepage

A homepage is what a browser opens by default whenever it is first launched. This is usually a page associated with the company that created the browser i.e. the Apple homepage for Safari. However, it is possible to customize the browser so that it opens with your own choice of homepage. To do this in Safari:

Don't forget

A unique Web page address is known as a URL. This stands for Uniform Resource Locator and means that every page on the Web is unique.

1 Open Safari and click on Safari>Preferences from the Menu bar

Safari	File	Edit	View

About Safari
Report Bugs to Apple...

Preferences...

2 Click on the General tab

General

3 Click on the Set to Current Page if you want the current page you are viewing to be your homepage

Set to Current Page

4 Enter a web address in the Home page box to set this as your homepage

Home page: http://www.apple.com

5 Click on this button to close the Preferences window

Using tabs

Safari was one of the first browsers to use tabs and this is still an integral part of its function.

Adding tabs
To add new tabs in Safari:

1 Select File>New Tab from the Menu bar

2 The new tab opens as a blank, untitled page

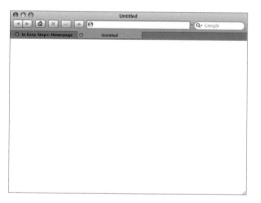

Don't forget

Tabs are usually a better option than opening a lot of different browser windows, as it keeps each new page within the same window.

109

3 Browse in the normal way in the new tab (the content in any other open tabs remains untouched)

4 To access, and change, shortcut keys for creating and using tabs, click on Safari> Preferences

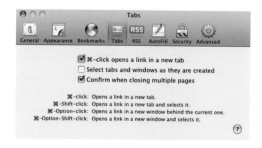

from the Menu bar and select the Tabs tab

Searching the Web

With the vast number of items on the Web it is essential to have a good search facility close at hand at all times. In Safari there is a Google search box built in to the toolbar. To use this:

1 The Google search box is located here

2 Type the required search keyword(s) and press Enter

3 The search results are displayed in the main browser window. Click on one to view that page

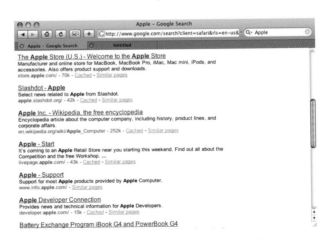

Adding bookmarks

Bookmarks in Safari are favorite pages to which you want to have regular, and fast, access. Bookmarks can be added to a bar at the top of the Safari window or a menu that is accessed from the Safari Menu bar.

Bookmarks Bar
To bookmark pages to the Bookmarks Bar:

1 Navigate to the page on the Web you want to bookmark

2 Click on this button on the Safari toolbar

3 Enter a name for the bookmarked page

4 Click here and select Bookmarks Bar

5 Click on the Add button

6 The page is added to the Bookmarks Bar. If it is not visible, select View>Show Bookmarks Bar from the Safari Menu bar. Click on a bookmark to move to that site

...cont'd

Bookmarks Menu

To bookmark pages to the Bookmarks Menu:

1 Navigate to the page on the Web you want to bookmark

2 Click on this button on the Safari toolbar

3 Enter a name for the bookmarked page

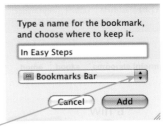

4 Click here and select Bookmarks Menu

5 Click on the Add button

6 To view the Bookmarks Menu, select Bookmarks from the Menu bar

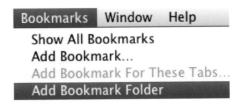

7 Click on the Add Bookmark Folder link if you want to create folders into which you can place your bookmarks, according to subject

Viewing your online history

In any Web session it is possible to look at dozens, or hundreds, of websites and pages. To make it easier to retrace your steps and return to previously viewed pages, the History option in Safari can be used. To do this:

1 Select History from the Safari Menu bar

History	Bookmarks	Window	Help
Back			
Forward			
Home			
Mark Page for SnapBack			
Page SnapBack			
Search Results SnapBack			
Reopen Last Closed Window			
Reopen All Windows From Last Session			
🐢 In Easy Steps: Homepage			

2 Click on an item here to return to a page that has been viewed in your current browsing session

3 Click on a date to view items that have been accessed previously

Monday, March 24, 2008
Sunday, March 23, 2008
Saturday, March 22, 2008
Friday, March 21, 2008

4 Click on Clear History to remove all of the items in your browsing history

Show All History
Clear History

Beware

If you clear your browsing history your browser will not remember any address that you have previously entered. If the history is not cleared, the browser will remember them as soon as you start typing the address.

Using SnapBack

Due to the number of pages and complexity of modern websites, it is sometimes possible to feel lost within them. Pages with useful information can sometimes get lost or forgotten once you have moved on from them. To overcome this Safari has a SnapBack function that enables you to quickly move back to particular pages within a site once you have identified them. To do this:

1 In Safari navigate to a page in a site

2 Select History>Mark Page for SnapBack from the Menu bar

History	Bookmarks	Window

Back
Forward
Home

Mark Page for SnapBack

3 When you move through pages on the rest of the site this icon appears in the Safari address bar

4 Click on the icon to move back to the page that was marked for SnapBack in Step 2

7 Being interactive online

This chapter shows some of the activities that can be undertaken on the Web. It covers buying items from online shops, delving into your family history, buying and selling on eBay and online games.

116 Shopping online

118 Booking a vacation

120 Researching family history

122 Price comparison sites

124 Shopping on eBay

127 Using online banking

128 Stocks and shares online

129 Maps online

130 Online games

Shopping online

The Web is a lot more than just a means of discovering facts and figures. It is also a means of doing business in terms of buying and selling. This can be for small or large purchases, but either way, online shopping has revolutionized our retail lives.

When you are shopping online there are some guidelines that should be followed to try and ensure you are in a safe online environment and do not spend too much money:

- Make a note of what you want to buy and stick to this once you have found it. Online shopping sites are adept at displaying a lot of enticing offers and it is a lot easier to buy something by clicking a button than it is to physically take it to a checkout

- Never buy anything that is promoted to you via an email, unless it is from a company who you have asked to send you promotional information

- When paying for items, make sure that the online site has a secure area for accepting payment and credit card details. A lot of sites display information about this within their payment area and another way to ascertain this is to check in the Address bar of the payment page. If it is within a secure area the address of the page will start with "https" rather than the standard "http"

a https://www.amazon.

Using online shopping

The majority of online shopping sites are similar in their operation:

- Goods are identified

- Goods are placed in a shopping basket

- Once the shopping is completed you proceed to the checkout

- You enter your shipping details and pay for the goods, usually with a credit card

On some sites you have to register before you can buy goods and in some cases this enables you to perform your shopping quicker by using a 1-click system. This means that all of your billing and payment details are already stored on the site and you can buy goods simply by clicking one button without having to re-enter your details. One of the most prominent sites to use this method is Amazon:

Beware

Be careful when shopping online as you can quickly get carried away since making purchases can be so easy.

Booking a vacation

Just as a lot of retailers have been creating an online presence, the same is also true for vacation companies and travel agents. It is now possible to book almost any type of vacation on the Web, from cruises to city breaks.

Several sites offer full travel services where they can deal with flights, hotels, insurance, car hire and excursions. These sites include:

- Expedia at www.expedia.com

- Travelocity at www.travelocity.com

- Tripadvisor at www.tripadvisor.com

These sites usually list special offers and last minute deals on their homepages and there is also a facility for specifying your precise requirements. To do this:

1 Select your vacation requirements

2 Enter flight details (if applicable)

3 Enter dates for your vacation

4 Click on the Search button

Create your trip

○ Flight only
○ Hotel only
○ Car only
Tour operator holidays

Tailor-make & SAVE!
⦿ Flight + Hotel
○ Flight + Hotel + Car
○ Flight + Car

Leaving from:

Going to:

(e.g. London or LGW)

(e.g. Costa del Sol or AGP)

Departing: Time: Returning: Time:
dd/mm/yy Anytii ▼   dd/mm/yy Anytii ▼

		Adults (19-64)	Children (0-18)	Seniors (65+)
Rooms: 1 ▼	Room 1	2 ▼	0 ▼	0 ▼

more flight + hotel search options:
More destinations...

(Search)

In addition to sites that do everything for you it is also possible to book your vacation on individual sites. This can be particularly useful for cruises and also for booking hotels around the world. Some websites to look at are:

Cruises

- Cruises.com at www.cruises.com

- Carnival at www.carnival.com

- Princess Cruises at www.princess.com

Don't forget

Vacation and hotel websites usually have versions that are specific to the geographical location in which you are situated.

119

Hotels

- Hotels.com at www.hotels.com

- All-hotels at www.all-hotels.com

- Choice Hotels International at www.choicehotels.com

Researching family history

A recent growth industry on the Web has been family history, or genealogy. Hundreds of organizations around the world have now digitized their records concerning individuals and family histories and there are numerous websites that provide online access to these records. Some of these sites are:

- Ancestry at www.ancestry.com

- Genealogy.com at www.genealogy.com

- Familysearch at www.familysearch.org

- RootsWeb.com at www.rootsweb.com

Most genealogy sites require you to register, for a fee, before you can conduct extensive family research on their sites, but once you do the process is similar on them all:

1 Enter the details of the family members in the search boxes

2 Click on the Search button

3 The results are displayed for the names searched against

Don't forget

Some sites offer a free initial search, but after that you will have to pay for each search.

4 On some sites there is a facility for creating your family tree. Enter the relevant details

5 Click on the Start Your Tree button

Price comparison sites

Everyone likes to get value for money when shopping or, better still, a bargain. On the Web it is possible to try and find the best possible prices for items before you buy them. This is done through price comparison sites that show the prices for items from a range of online retailers. Some of the price comparison sites include:

- PriceGrabber at www.pricegrabber.com

- PriceRunner at www.pricerunner.com

- ActiveShopper at www.activeshopper.com

To use a price comparison site:

Don't forget

Price comparison sites do not actually sell anything: they just direct you to different retailers.

1 Select one of the online price comparison sites

2 Select a category for the type of product you want to buy

Cameras & Camcorders
Digital Cameras, Camcorders, Memory Cards, More...

3 Locate the product you want to buy

⊕ Enlarge image

Compare prices : **Canon EOS Elan 7NE**
More product info

Price range: $349.95 - $616
User rating: Write review
Expert rating: ▮▮▮▮▮▮▮▮▮▮ 1 Expert review

4 Click on the Compare Prices link or tab

Compare prices

5 The available retailers and their prices are displayed

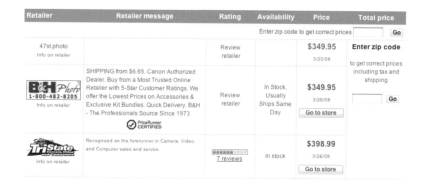

Retailer	Retailer message	Rating	Availability	Price	Total price
					Enter zip code to get correct prices [ ] Go
47st.photo Info on retailer		Review retailer		$349.95 3/25/08	Enter zip code to get correct prices including tax and shipping
B&H Photo 1-800-482-8205 Info on retailer	SHIPPING from $6.65. Canon Authorized Dealer. Buy from a Most Trusted Online Retailer with 5-Star Customer Ratings. We offer the Lowest Prices on Accessories & Exclusive Kit Bundles. Quick Delivery. B&H - The Professionals Source Since 1973. PriceRunner CERTIFIED	Review retailer	In Stock, Usually Ships Same Day	$349.95 3/26/08 Go to store	[ ] Go
TriState Info on retailer	Recognized as the forerunner in Camera, Video, and Computer sales and service. 7 reviews		In stock	$398.99 3/26/08 Go to store	

6 Click on a retailer's link or icon to go to their site, from where the item can be purchased

Shopping on eBay

eBay is one of the phenomenon of the online world. Started as a small site in California it has grown into a multi-billion business with online auctions and also standard online retailer transactions. To buy and sell items on eBay you have to be registered. This can be done from the eBay homepage by clicking on the Register button or link. This takes you through the registration process, which is free.

Buying items

Once you have registered you can start buying and selling items. In some ways it is better to start by buying some cheaper items just to get used to the system. To do this:

Beware

Most people are honest on eBay but you do sometimes get unscrupulous buyers and sellers.

1 To find items to buy, enter a keyword in the search box and click on the Search button, or

> Ancient coins
>
> Search

2 Click on the Categories button and drill down through the various categories

> **Shop your Favorite Categories**
>
> Antiques
> Art
> Baby
> Books
> Business & Industrial
> Cameras & Photo
> Cars, Boats, Vehicles & Parts
> Cell Phones & PDAs
> Clothing, Shoes & Accessories
> Coins & Paper Money
> Collectibles
> Computers & Networking
> Consumer Electronics
> Crafts
> Dolls & Bears
> DVDs & Movies

3 When you find items in which you are interested, select whether you want to view them according to Auctions, Buy It Now (single price purchase) or both

> **All Items** | **Auctions** | **Buy It Now**

4 Click on an item to view its details LOT ANCIENT ROMAN COINS & PIRATE GOLD DOUBLOON REPROS

5 For Buy It Now items, click on this button to purchase the item

Buy It Now >

6 For auction items, enter a bid in the Place Bid box and click on the Place Bid button

Starting bid: **US $14.95**

Your maximum bid: **US $** [15.00]   Place Bid >

(Enter US $14.95 or more)

7 Review the item and purchase details

Review and Confirm Bid

Hello nickvan1! (Not you?)

 Item you're bidding on:
LOT ANCIENT ROMAN COINS & PIRATE GOLD DOUBLOON REPROS
Current bid: US $14.95
Your maximum bid: **US $15.00**

Sales Tax: 8.250% (only in CA)
Shipping and handling: To United Kingdom -- US $7.95 -- Standard Int'l Flat Rate Shipping.
Shipping insurance: US $1.35(Optional)
Payment methods: PayPal, Personal check, Money order/Cashiers check.

8 If you want to proceed with your bid, click on the Confirm Bid button

Confirm Bid

9 If you are successful in the auction you will be notified on eBay and also via email. At this point you pay the vendor for the item and they should mail it to you

 Don't forget

Once you have completed the transaction you can leave feedback about the seller.

...cont'd

Selling items

If you want to sell items on eBay you have to first list them for sale. To do this:

1 Click on the Sell button at the top of the eBay window

2 Enter a short description of your item

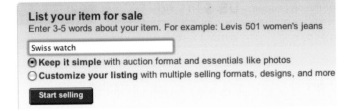

126

3 Click on the Start Selling button

Start selling

4 Complete the wizard for selling items. This includes a detailed description of the item and photographs

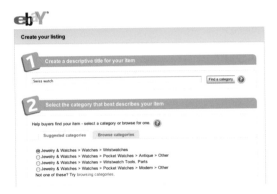

5 Once the wizard has been completed the item will be listed in the relevant category on eBay

Using online banking

Online banking has helped to transform our financial activities in the same way as online shopping has transformed our retail ones. Most major banks have online banking facilities and they can be used for a number of services, including:

- Managing your accounts
- Transferring money
- Pay bills
- Applying for credit cards
- Paying credit cards
- Applying for loans

Before you can use any of these online services you have to first register and apply for an online account:

1 On the homepage of most bank websites there are boxes for signing in if you are an existing online customer or applying for a new account. Select the relevant option and you will then be taken through the necessary steps

Sign on to your account

Choose one

Apply for a new account

Choose one

✓ Choose one
Access Account
Checking
Ultimate Money Account
Ultimate Savings Account
Savings
Certificate of Deposit (CD)
Credit Card
IRA
Home Equity Line/Loan
Mortgage
Student Loan

Stocks and shares online

An extension of online banking is being able to deal in stocks and shares on the Web. You can buy and sell on the stock market without having to leave the comfort of your own home. A number of financial services websites offer this facility and they also provide a lot of background information as well as the buying and selling function. If you are going to be trading stocks and shares on the Web it is a good idea to find out as much about them before you start trading. In this respect the websites of relevant stock markets provide a very useful source of information:

1 Enter details to get current stock prices

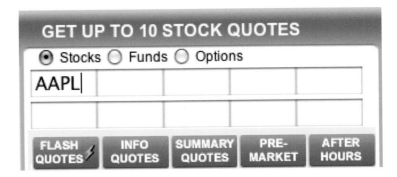

2 Use the Research areas to find out the history and performance of individual stocks and shares

Quotes, Charts & Research

3 Check the latest Market News for tips and warnings

Market News

Beware

Never buy stocks and shares from any offers you receive by email.

Maps online

Maps have fascinated mankind for thousands of years and with the Web it has never been easier to view local, national or international maps. In addition, the sites that provide these services also provide a host of additional information about hotels, airports, schools and civic amenities. Two sites to look at for maps are:

- Multimap at www. multimap.com

- Google Maps at http://maps.google.com

To use an online mapping service:

1 Enter a name or zip code of somewhere you want to look up

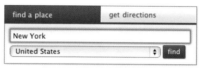

2 The results display the required map

Don't forget

Online mapping services can also provide directions between two different locations.

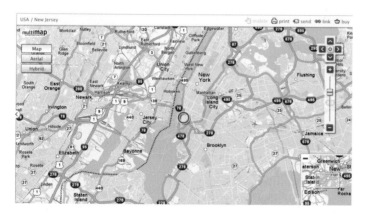

3 Use this slider to zoom in or out of the map

Online games

Online gambling has developed in some countries in recent years but it is also possible to play online games, such as bridge and backgammon, without the need to gamble away your life savings. Although some of these sites do allow you to play for money, others offer a less financially pressurized environment. For both bridge and backgammon sites you can either play against the computer or other people who are on the site. Either way, you are usually presented with a graphic interface of the action:

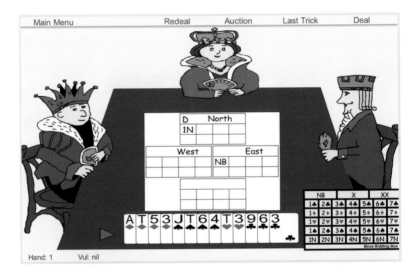

8 Keeping in touch

Communication, as much as money, makes the world go round. This chapter shows how to use the Mac tools to communicate by email, text and video.

132   Setting up email

133   Adding mailboxes

134   Creating email

136   Attaching photos

138   Email stationery

139   Dealing with junk email

140   Text and video chatting

Setting up email

Email is an essential element for most computer users and Macs come with their own email program called Mail. This covers all of the email functionality that anyone could need.

When first using Mail you have to set up your email account. This information will be available from the company who provides your email service, although in some cases Mail may obtain this information automatically. To view your Mail account details:

1 Click on this icon on the Dock

2 Select Mail>Preferences from the Menu bar

3 Click on the Accounts tab

4 If it has not already been included, enter the details of your email account in the Account Information section

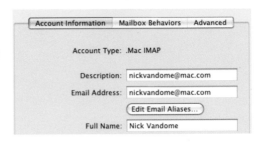

5 Click on this button to close the Mail Preferences window

Adding mailboxes

Before you start creating email messages it is a good idea to create a folder structure (mailboxes) for your emails. This will allow you to sort your emails into relevant subjects when you receive them, rather than having all of them sitting in your Inbox. To add new mailboxes:

1 Mailboxes are displayed in the Mailboxes panel

2 At the bottom of the Mailboxes panel, click on this icon **+**

Don't forget

Different mailboxes can be used to store emails according to their subject matter.

3 Select where you want the mailbox to be created (by default this will be On My Mac)

4 Enter a name for the new mailbox

5 Click on the OK button

6 The new mailbox is added to the current list

Creating email

Mail enables you to send and receive emails and also format them to your own style. This can be simply formatting text or adding customized stationery.

To access Mail and start creating email messages:

1 Click on this icon on the Dock

2 Mail contains options for creating, receiving and formatting email messages

3 Click on this button to create a new email message

4 Enter the email address of the recipient in the To box

To: robin.vandome@mac.com

5 Enter a title for the email in the Subject box

Subject: Well done

6 Enter the content for the email here

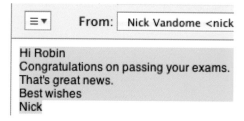

Hi Robin
Congratulations on passing your exams.
That's great news.
Best wishes
Nick

7 To format the text in the email, select it first

From: Nick Vandome <nick

Hi Robin
Congratulations on passing your exams.
That's great news.
Best wishes
Nick

8 Click on the Fonts button

Fonts

9 Select formatting options for the text

Hot tip

Select a reasonably large font size to ensure that your email can be read easily.

135

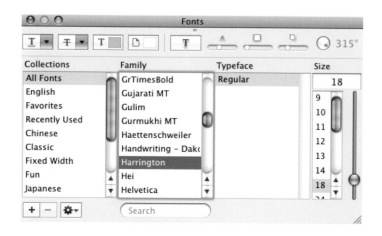

10 Click on the Send button to send the email to the selected recipient

Send

Attaching photos

Emails do not have to be restricted to plain text. Through the use of attachments they can also include other documents and particularly photos. This is an excellent way to send photos to family and friends around the world. There are two ways to attach photos to an email:

Attach button
To attach photos using the Attach button:

Beware

Do not send files that are too large in terms of file size, otherwise the recipient may find it takes too long to download.

1 Click on this icon on the Mail toolbar

2 Browse your hard drive for the photo(s) you want to include in your email. Select the photos you want

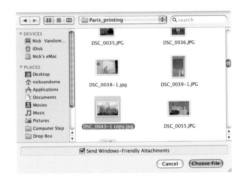

3 Click on the Choose File button

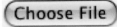

4 The photo is added to the body of the email

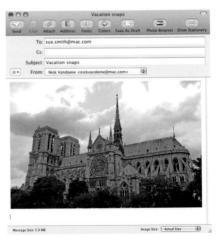

Photo Browser

To attach photos using the Photo Browser:

1 Click on this icon on the Mail toolbar

2 Browse the Photo Browser for the photo(s) that you want to include

Don't forget

The Photo Browser is available from a variety of other applications.

3 Drag the selected photo(s) into the open email to include them in the message

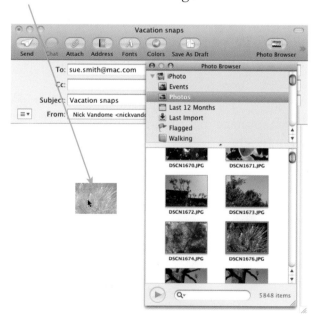

Email stationery

You do not have to settle for conservative formatting options in emails and Mail offers a variety of templates that can give your messages a creative and eye-catching appearance. It can also be used to format any photos that you have attached to your message. This is done through the use of the Stationery function. To use this:

1 Click on this icon on the Mail toolbar

2 Select a category for the stationery

3 Double-click on a style to apply it to the email

4 The stationery incorporates any photos that have been attached

Dealing with junk email

Spam, or junk email, is the scourge of every email user. It is unwanted and unsolicited messages that are usually sent in bulk to lists of email addresses. In Mail there is a function to try and limit the amount of junk email that you receive in your Inbox. To do this:

1 When you receive a junk email, click on this button on the Mail toolbar (initially this will help to train Mail to identify junk email)

2 Once Mail has recognized the types of junk that you receive it will start to filter them directly into the Junk Mailbox

Hot tip

It is worth occasionally checking in your Junk Mailbox, in case something you want has been put there.

3 To set the preferences for junk email select Mail>Preferences from the Menu bar and click on the Junk tab

4 Junk email is displayed in the Junk Mailbox

•	⚑	From	Subject
○		WebProNews	If They're Searching, Give ...
●		Maricela Goddard	Let yourself look really swell!

Text and video chatting

One issue with email is that you can never be sure when the recipient receives the message, or when they will reply to it. For a more immediate form of communication, instant message or video messaging can be used. This is done with the iChat program. To use this:

1 Click on this icon on the Dock

Hot tip

If you want to make telephone calls from your Mac, try the program Skype at www.skype.com. This can be used to make free phone calls to other Skype users.

2 In order to chat to someone you have to add them as a buddy. To do this, click on this button

3 Select the required contact from your Address book

4 Select a buddy in the iChat window

5 Click on this button to start a text chat

6 Click on this button to start a video chat

9 Sharing online

Macs are a lot more than just computers and Apple have worked to create a joined-up digital world. This chapter shows how the online .Mac service can be used to expand your Mac horizons.

142 Sharing with .Mac

144 Creating an iDisk

146 iDisk preferences

147 Synchronizing with .Mac

148 Sharing photos online

151 Viewing a Web Gallery

152 Creating your own website

156 Sending iCards

158 Creating a group

Sharing with .Mac

Some companies make computers and some companies run online services for email and sharing files. However, Apple does both: their .Mac online sharing service is closely integrated so that sharing items online is virtually the same as working with them on your Mac computer. There is an annual subscription fee for .Mac but for this you get:

- An online email account that you can synchronize with your Mac computer

- An online version of your Mac Address Book

- An option for creating your own website

- Online greeting cards

- Online disk space for storage or backing up

- Bookmarks that you have set up on your Mac

- Groups to which you can invite friends and family members

To join .Mac and start using its services:

Don't forget

.Mac probably contains all of the services you will need for interacting online.

142

1 Go to the .Mac homepage at www.apple.com/dotmac/

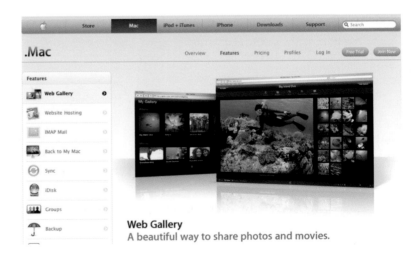

Web Gallery
A beautiful way to share photos and movies.

2 Click on the Free Trial or the Join Now button

3 For both options in Step 2 you will have to register.
The Free Trial is for 60 days, while the normal sign
up involves paying the annual subscription fee (at the
time of writing this is US$99.95 for an individual
annual membership)

.mac   Sign up for a 60 day free trial

To sign up for your free trial, please provide the following information and click Continue.

Personal Information

First Name   Last Name

Current Email Address

Country   Language
United States   English

Member Name and Password

Choose a Member Name (3-20 characters)   Password (6-32 characters)

@mac.com

Your member name will also be your email name and   Password (confirm)
cannot be changed after sign-up.

Don't forget

Once you have
subscribed to the
full .Mac service your
subscription will be
debited automatically
each year unless you
specify for it to stop.
You will receive an
email about a month
before, telling you the
date of payment.

143

4 Once you have registered, click on the Mail button
to access your online email

Mail   0   ✉

---

5 Once you are signed up for .Mac this email account
will be available on your Mac computer too. The
.Mac email enables you to access your email from
any Internet enabled computer in the world

Creating an iDisk

iDisk is a function of .Mac that effectively enables you to have a backup hard drive online. The basic .Mac membership gives you 10 Gb of storage on your iDisk.

iDisk can be used to back up your files and it is possible to access files on iDisk from any Internet enabled computer. To use iDisk:

1 When you register for .Mac the iDisk icon will appear in the Finder

2 Select a file or folder that you want to include on your iDisk

3 Select File>Copy from the Finder Menu bar

4 Double-click on the iDisk icon and locate a folder into which you want to place the file or folder

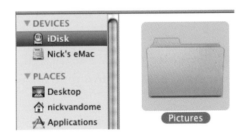

5 Select File>Paste from the Finder Menu bar

6 Once you have added files or folders to your iDisk icon in the Finder these will automatically be copied to your online iDisk on .Mac (as long as you have an active Internet connection)

Viewing your iDisk online

To view the contents of your iDisk from within .Mac:

1 Access the .Mac homepage and log in to your account

2 In the .Mac panel scroll down until you see the iDisk icon. Click on it

3 The contents of your iDisk are displayed. Double-click on a folder to display its contents

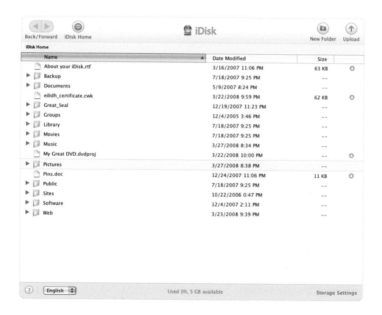

4 Click on this icon next to a file to download it onto whichever computer you are accessing it from

iDisk preferences

Within the System Preferences folder it is possible to determine how iDisk works on your Mac. To do this:

1 Click on the System Preferences icon on the Dock

2 In the System Preferences folder, click on the .Mac icon

.Mac

3 Click on the iDisk tab   iDisk

4 This scale shows how much iDisk space you have used up

iDisk Usage

| 0 | 2.48 GB | 4.95 GB |

5 Click on the Upgrade Storage button to go online to purchase more iDisk space from .Mac

Upgrade Storage...

Beware

If you allow Read and Write access to your iDisk Public Folder this means that other people will be able to edit the files contained in this folder.

6 Select how you want other people to be able to access your Public Folder within iDisk

Your iDisk Public Folder

You can connect to your iDisk public folder at http://idisk.mac.com/nickvandome

Allow others to: ● Read only   ○ Read and Write

☐ Password-protect your public folder

Synchronizing with .Mac

One of the potential problems with having the copies of the same files on your computer and on the .Mac site is that there is the potential for them to become unsynchronized if you update one version and not the other. This is overcome by the synchronization function which ensures that the relevant information on your computer and your .Mac account are both synchronized. This means that wherever you access your .Mac account from you can be sure that it is the same information as on your Mac computer. To do this:

1 Click on the System Preferences icon on the Dock

2 Click on the .Mac icon (as on the previous page)

3 Click on the Sync tab

4 Check on the items you want synchronized

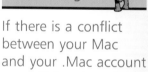
Don't forget

If there is a conflict between your Mac and your .Mac account you will be alerted to the fact and asked how you would like to resolve it.

5 Check on this box to have your Mac computer and .Mac account synchronized automatically

6 Click on the Sync Now button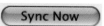

Sharing photos online

.Mac is a great environment in which to share your photos and videos online. This is done by uploading them into a Web Gallery in your .Mac account. You can then invite family and friends to come and view them. To do this:

1 Click on the iPhoto icon on the Dock

2 In iPhoto select the photos you want to use in the Web Gallery

Don't forget

Other people do not have to be .Mac members in order for them to be able to view your Web Gallery.

3 Click on the Web Gallery button

Web Gallery

4 Set preferences for how you would like people to view and use your Web Gallery

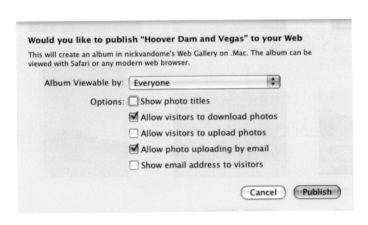

Would you like to publish "Hoover Dam and Vegas" to your Web

This will create an album in nickvandome's Web Gallery on .Mac. The album can be viewed with Safari or any modern web browser.

Album Viewable by: Everyone

Options: ☐ Show photo titles
☑ Allow visitors to download photos
☐ Allow visitors to upload photos
☑ Allow photo uploading by email
☐ Show email address to visitors

Cancel Publish

5 Click on the Publish button

6 Click on the link at the top of the iPhoto window to go to your .Mac Web Gallery

7 The Web Gallery is published within your .Mac account

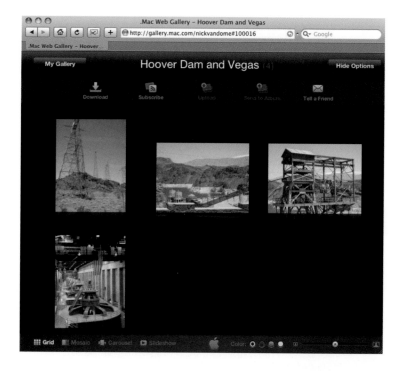

8 Click on the Tell a Friend button to invite other people to view your Web Gallery

9 Enter your email address

From: nickvandome@mac.com

10 Enter the recipient's email address

To: brianjones@mac.com

11 Enter a message

Message: Hi Brian
Here are some photos from our recent trip to
Vegas and the Hoover Dam. Great!

12 Enter the visible code

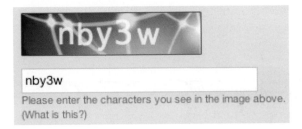

nby3w

Please enter the characters you see in the image above.
(What is this?)

13 Click on the Send button

Send

Viewing a Web Gallery

When you invite someone to view one of your Web
Galleries they receive an email with the following message:

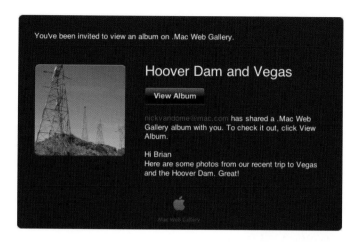

When they click on the View Album
button they will be taken straight to
the appropriate Gallery:

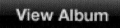

Hot tip

Images can be viewed
at different sizes in
a Web Gallery by
dragging the slider in
the bottom right-hand
corner of the Web
Gallery window.

Creating your own website

It seems as if everybody has their own websites these days. Not only are they a great way to publish family information, they are also ideal for clubs or charity organizations. With .Mac and a program called iWeb it is possible to quickly get up and running on the Web with your own site. To do this:

1 Click on the iWeb icon on the Dock, or select it in the Applications folder

2 Select a template for the design of your website

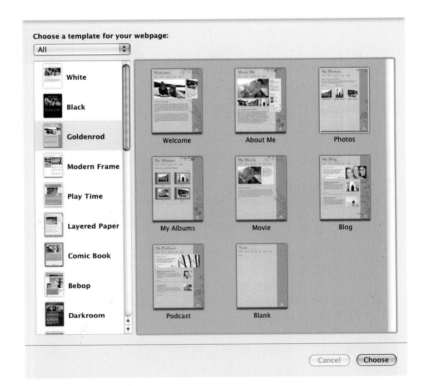

Choose a template for your webpage:

All

White

Black

Goldenrod

Modern Frame

Play Time

Layered Paper

Comic Book

Bebop

Darkroom

Welcome | About Me | Photos
My Albums | Movie | Blog
Podcast | Blank

Cancel   Choose

3 Click on the Choose button

4 Click on a text item and overtype to change it

5 Click on the Media button at the bottom of the window

6 Click on the Photos tab and select a photo

Beware

Photos can be resized on an iWeb page, but do not make them too big or else they may take up too much space on the screen.

7 Drag the photo onto one of the existing photo placeholders

Coffee by the water

...cont'd

8 Your own photo replaces the current item

DSC_0568.JPG

9 Click on this button to change the theme for the page

Theme

10 Click on this button to add a text box (by dragging) on the page

Text Box

11 Click on this button to add shapes to the page

Shapes

12 To add a new page, select File>New Page from the iWeb Menu bar, or click on the Add button under the Site panel

13 In the Site panel, click on the names of each page to move between them

14 Click on the Publish button to publish the site to your .Mac account

15 The following message will appear. Click on Continue

16 Once your website has been published the following message appears

Don't forget

The web address of your site will automatically start with http://web.mac. com, followed by your own .Mac username.

155

17 Click on the Announce button to invite family and friends to view your site

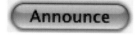

18 An email is generated with this message pre-inserted. Add email recipients and send the message to them. When they receive it they will be able to follow a link to your website

Hi everyone,

I just updated my website and thought you might want to check it out. To visit, just click on the links below or paste the URLs into your browser.

Site http://web.mac.com/nickvandome
Photos
My Albums

Take a look and let me know what you think!

Sending iCards

iCards is a .Mac function with which you can send electronic greeting cards to friends and family. To do this:

1 Access the .Mac homepage and log in to your account

2 In the .Mac panel scroll down until you see the iCards icon. Click on it

3 The categories of the available iCards are displayed

4 Click on the photo you want to use for your iCard

Taste Tester

5 On the next page, select a style of writing for the card

 Select a type style for your card:

⦿Calligraphy ○*Fancy*

○Casual ○Classic

○Modern ○FUN

6 Enter the message for the card

 Write your message here:
(Your text will re-size to fit the message area.)

Just wanted to send you some birthday wishes!

7 Click on the Continue button

CONTINUE

8 On the next page, enter your name and email address

Your Information:

Enter your name
Nick Vandome

Enter your email
nickvandome@mac.com

Don't forget

When you are sending an iCard you can also send a copy to yourself.

157

9 Enter the recipient's email address

Enter emails, separated by commas
petervandome@mac.com

10 Check the card and click on the Send Card button

Just wanted to send you some birthday wishes!

SEND CARD

Creating a group

Groups on .Mac are collaborative areas where groups of people can view and share files. To join a group you have to have a .Mac ID, although you do not have to still be an active .Mac member. To create a group:

1 Log in to your .Mac account and click on the Groups link

2 Click on the Create a New Group button

3 Enter details for the Group

4 Click on the Submit button

Submit

5 Access your Group in your .Mac account

Nick's test
http://groups.mac.com/nickv1

Owner   Edit

6 Within the Members' area, click on the Invite link to invite new members

Members

Search

Nick Vandome

Invite or Manage

10 Expanding your horizons

This chapter shows how you can develop your skills on a Mac, from adding new users to setting up a network of computers.

160 Adding users

162 Login options

164 Switching between users

165 Parental controls

170 Creating your own network

173 Sharing on a network

Adding users

Due to the power and versatility of Macs it would seem a shame to limit their use to a single person. Thankfully, it is possible to set up user accounts for several people on the same Mac. This means that each person can log in to their own settings and preferences. All user accounts can be password protected, to ensure that each user's environment is secure. To set up multiple user accounts:

1 Click on the System Preferences icon on the Dock

2 Click on the Accounts icon

Don't forget

Each user can select their own icon or photo of themselves.

3 The information about the current account is displayed. This is your own account and the information is based on details you provide when you first set up your Mac

4 Click on this icon to enable new accounts to be added (the padlock needs to be open)

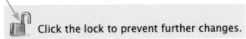

Click the lock to prevent further changes.

...cont'd

5 Click on the plus sign icon to add a new account

6 Enter the details for the new account holder

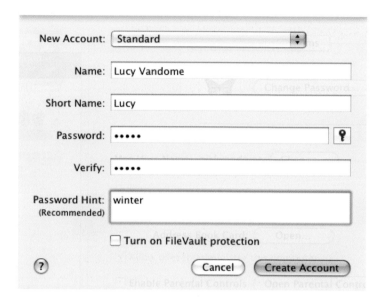

7 Click on the Create Account button

8 The new account is added to the list in the Accounts window, under Other Accounts

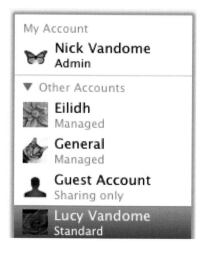

Don't forget

By default, you are the administrator of your own Mac. This means that you can create, edit and delete other user accounts.

161

Login options

Once you have set up more than one user you can determine what happens at login i.e. when the Mac is turned on. You may want to display a list of all of the users for that machine, or you may want to have yourself logged in automatically. To set login options:

1 Click on the System Preferences icon on the Dock

2 Click on the Accounts icon

Accounts

3 Click on the padlock to open it

4 Click on the Login Options button

Login Options

5 The Login Options window allows you to select settings for when you turn on your Mac

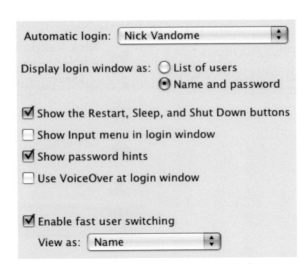

Automatic login: Nick Vandome

Display login window as: ○ List of users
                               ● Name and password

☑ Show the Restart, Sleep, and Shut Down buttons
☐ Show Input menu in login window
☑ Show password hints
☐ Use VoiceOver at login window

☑ Enable fast user switching
     View as: Name

6 Click on the Automatic Login box

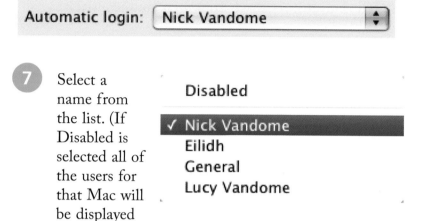

Automatic login: Nick Vandome

If Automatic Login is selected for a named user, no username or password needs to be selected when the Mac is turned on.

7 Select a name from the list. (If Disabled is selected all of the users for that Mac will be displayed at login)

Disabled

✓ Nick Vandome
Eilidh
General
Lucy Vandome

8 If Disabled is selected, select one of the options for how the login window is displayed

Display login window as: ● List of users
                         ○ Name and password

9 Check on this box if you want to make it as easy as possible to switch between users (see next page)

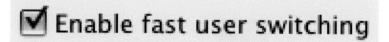

☑ Enable fast user switching

Switching between users

If there are multiple users set up on a Mac it is useful to be able to switch between them as quickly as possible. When this is done, the first user's session is retained so that they can return to it if required. To switch between users:

1 Make sure Fast User Switching is enabled (see previous page)

☑ Enable fast user switching

2 At the top-right of the screen, click on the current user's name

Nick Vandome

3 Click on the name of another user

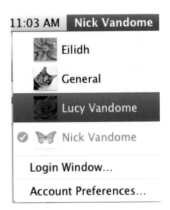
11:03 AM   Nick Vandome

🌼 Eilidh

🐱 General

Lucy Vandome

✔ 🦋 Nick Vandome

Login Window...

Account Preferences...

4 Enter the relevant password (if required)

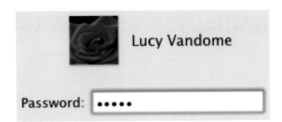
Lucy Vandome

Password: •••••

5 Click on the Log In button

Log In

Parental controls

Children, and grandchildren, love computers and it is not always possible to fully monitor what they are doing on them. Therefore, it is useful to be able to put in some system controls if you have any user accounts for younger members of the family. To do this:

1 Click on the System Preferences icon on the Dock

2 Click on the Parental Controls icon

Parental
Controls

Don't forget

Different types of parental controls can be set for each user account on a Mac.

3 Select a user account to which you want to apply controls. By default, Parental Controls are turned off

Parental controls are turned off for this account.

Parental controls let you manage your child's use of this computer, the applications on it, and the Internet.

(**Enable Parental Controls**)

4 Click on this button to enable Parental Controls

(**Enable Parental Controls**)

...cont'd

System controls

1 Click on the System tab

2 Check on the Use Simple Finder box to show a simplified version of the Finder

 ☑ **Use Simple Finder**
Provides a simplified view of the computer desktop for young or inexperienced users.

3 Check on this box if you want to limit the types of program that a user can access

 ☑ **Only allow selected applications**
Allows user to open only the selected applications. An administrator's password is required to open other applications.

4 Check off the boxes next to the programs that you do not want used

Check the applications to allow

▶ ☐ iLife
▶ ☑ iWork
▼ ⊟ Internet
　　☐ 🌐 Explorer
　　☐ 💬 iChat
　　☑ ✉ Mail
　　☑ 🧭 Safari

Content controls

1 Click on the Content tab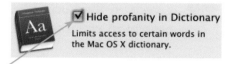

2 Check on this box to prevent any profanities in the Mac Dictionary being displayed

3 Click on this button and click on the Customize button to edit the type of Web content that can be viewed

4 Enter the Web addresses for sites that are acceptable

Always allow these sites:
http://www.ineasysteps.com

5 Enter the Web addresses for sites that are not acceptable

Never allow these sites:
http://www.badcontent.com

6 Click on the OK button OK

...cont'd

Mail and iChat controls

1. Click on the Mail & iChat tab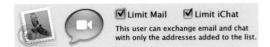

2. Check on the Limit boxes to limit the type of content in email messages and iChat text messages

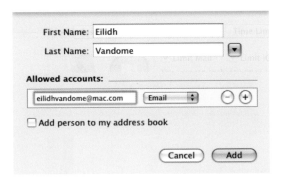

3. Click on this button to enter the names of people who are acceptable for exchanging emails and iChat messages with the user

4. Enter the names of people who are acceptable for exchanging emails and iChat messages with the user

| First Name: | Eilidh |
| Last Name: | Vandome |

Allowed accounts:

eilidhvandome@mac.com   Email

Add person to my address book

Cancel   Add

5. Click on the Add button

6. Check on this box if you want to be notified when someone not on the list in Step 3 tries to make contact with the user

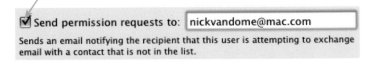
Send permission requests to: nickvandome@mac.com
Sends an email notifying the recipient that this user is attempting to exchange email with a contact that is not in the list.

Time controls

1 Click on the Time Limits tab   **Time Limits**

2 Check on this box to limit the amount of time the user can use the Mac

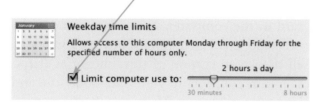

3 Check on these boxes to determine the times at which the user cannot access their account

Log controls

1 Click on the Logs tab   **Logs**

2 The logs can be edited to show activity over a certain time period and content type

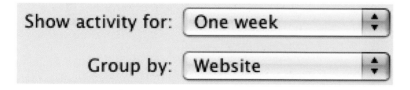

Creating your own network

Computer networks are two or more computers joined together to share information. A computer connected to the Internet constitutes a network, as does one computer connected to another.

Networks can be set up by joining computers together with cables or wirelessly. The latter is becoming more and more common and this can be done with a wireless router and a wireless card in the computer. New Macs come with wireless cards installed so it is just a case of buying a wireless router. (Apple sell their own version of this, known as Airport.) A wireless router connects to your telephone line and then you can set up your Mac, or Macs, to join the network and communicate with each other and the Internet. To do this:

Don't forget

Wireless routers should automatically detect a wireless card in a Mac.

1 Click on the System Preferences icon on the Dock

2 Click on the Network icon

3 The Network window displays the current settings

4 Click on the Assist Me button

5 The Network Setup Assistant is launched

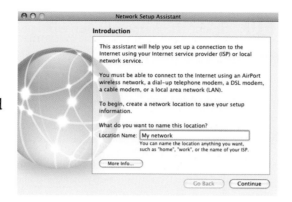

6 Enter a name for your network connection

What do you want to name this location?

Location Name: | My network |

You can name the location anything you want, such as "home", "work", or the name of your ISP.

7 Click on the Continue button   **Continue**

8 Select how you connect to the Internet

How Do You Connect to the Internet?

Please select the method you use to connect to the Internet:

- ⦿ I use AirPort to connect to the Internet wirelessly.
- ◯ I use a telephone modem to dial my ISP.
- ◯ I use a DSL modem to connect to the Internet.

9 Click on the Continue button   **Continue**

...cont'd

10 Select the name of your wireless router

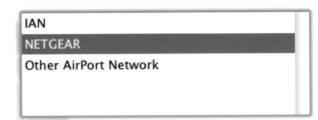

Beware

In the wireless network window you may see other available networks. This could be because you are in receiving distance of your neighbor's wireless network. Do not try to connect to this as there can be legal implications.

11 Enter the password for the router. This will have been set when you installed the router

Password: Selected network requires a password

••••••••

12 Click on the Continue button   **Continue**

13 The Ready to Connect window confirms that you are ready to connect to your router

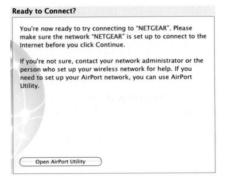

14 Click on the Continue button   **Continue**

Sharing on a network

One of the main reasons for creating a network of two or more computers is to share files between them. On networked Macs, this involves setting them up so that they can share files and then accessing these files.

Setting up file sharing
To set up file sharing on a networked Mac:

1 Click on the System Preference icon on the Dock

2 Click on the Sharing icon

Sharing

3 Check on the boxes next to the items you want to share (the most common items to share are files and printers)

On	Service
☐	Screen Sharing
☑	File Sharing
☑	Printer Sharing
☐	Web Sharing
☐	Remote Login
☐	Remote Management
☐	Remote Apple Events
☐	Xgrid Sharing
☐	Internet Sharing

173

Don't forget

If you only use your network to connect to the Internet then you do not need to worry about file sharing. This is mainly for sharing files between two different computers.

4 Click on the padlock to close it and prevent more changes

...cont'd

Accessing other computers

When you access other computers on a network you do so as either a registered user or a guest. If you are a registered user it usually means you are accessing another computer of which you are an administrator i.e. the main user. This gives you greater access to the computer's contents than if you are a guest. To access another computer on your network:

1 Networked computers should show up automatically in the Finder. Double-click on one to access it

2 By default, you will be connected as a Guest, with limited access. Click on the Connect As button in the Finder window

3 Click on Registered User button

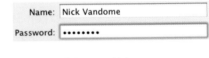

4 Enter your name and the password for the computer to which you want to connect (this will be your user password on that computer)

Don't forget

When connecting to another computer, it has to be turned on.

5 Click on the Connect button

6 In the Finder you will have access to the hard drive of the networked computer

7 You will then be able to access files and folders in the same way as if they were on the computer on which you are viewing them

Guest users

Guest users on a network are users other than yourself, or other registered users, to whom you want to limit access to your files and folders. Guests only have access to a folder called the Drop Box in your own Public folder. To share files with Guest users you have to first copy them into the Drop Box. To do this:

1 Create a file and select File>Save from the Menu bar

2 Navigate to your own home folder (this is created automatically by OS X and displayed in the Finder Sidebar)

Don't forget

Your home folder is the one with your Mac username.

3 Double-click on the Public folder

Public

4 Double-click on the Drop Box folder

Drop Box

5 Save the file into the Drop Box

Shared Folder

PAGES

network_test

...cont'd

Accessing a Drop Box
To access files in a Drop Box:

1 Double-click on a networked computer in the Finder

2 Click on the Connect As button in the Finder window

3 Click on the Guest button

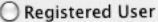

176

4 Click on the Connect button

5 Double-click on the administrator's folder

6 Double-click on the Drop Box folder to access the files within it

11 Safety net

This chapter shows some of the ways in which you can keep your Mac, and your files, safe and secure.

178 Mac security

179 Updating software

180 Checking your system

183 Dealing with crashes

184 Backing up

Mac security

Modern computers are plagued by viruses, spyware and malware, all of which can corrupt data or impair the smooth running of the system. Thankfully, Macs are less prone to this than computers running Windows, partly due to the fact that there are a smaller number of Macs for the virus writers to worry about and partly because the UNIX system on which the Mac OS X is based is a very robust platform.

However, this is not to say that Mac users should be complacent in the face of potential attacks. In order to try and minimize the threat of viruses and unwanted visitors try some of the following steps:

- Install anti-virus software and a firewall. Although this is not as essential as for a computer running Windows it will give you additional peace of mind. Norton and Sophos produce good anti-virus software for the Mac

- Protect your Mac with a password. This means that no-one can log on without the required password

- Download software updates from Apple, which, among other things, contain security updates (see next page)

- Do not open suspicious email attachments

- In Safari, select Safari>Preferences and click on the Security tab. Deselect any items that you feel may put your computer at risk

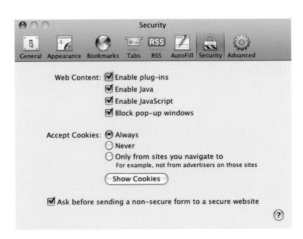

Updating software

Apple periodically releases updates for its software: both its programs and the OS X operating system. The latter are probably more important as they contain security fixes for the system that have come to light. To update software:

1 Click on the System Preferences icon on the Dock

2 Click on the Software Update icon

Software
Update

3 Click on the Check Now button to view available updates

Check Now

4 Check on the boxes next to the updates you want to install

Install	Name	Version	Size
☑	Pages Update	3.0.2	29.2 MB
☑	Numbers Update	1.0.2	27.4 MB
☑	iTunes	7.6.1	44.1 MB
☑	iWeb Update	2.0.3	18.4 MB
☑	iPhoto Update	7.1.2	15.9 MB
☐	Front Row Update	2.1.2	17.2 MB
☐	AirPort Utility	5.3.1	10.6 MB
☑	Mac OS X Update	10.5.2	341 MB

5 Click on the Install button

Install 10 Items

6 Check on the Check for Updates box to have updates checked for automatically

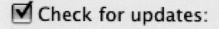 

Don't forget

If checks are set automatically, you will be alerted, at the specified time, whenever updates are available and you can choose whether to install them or not.

Checking your system

Macs have a couple of programs that can be used to check the overall health and condition of your system. These are utilities called Activity Monitor and System Profiler. To access these programs:

1 In the Finder, click on the Applications button

2 Double-click on the Utilities folder

3 Double-click on either program to open it

Activity Monitor

This can be used to check how much memory is being used up on your Mac, and also by certain programs:

1 Click on the CPU tab to see how much processor memory is being used up

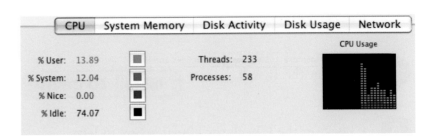

2 Click on the System Memory tab to see how much system memory (RAM) is being used up

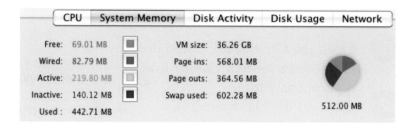

3 Click on the Disk Usage tab to see how much space has been taken up on the hard drive

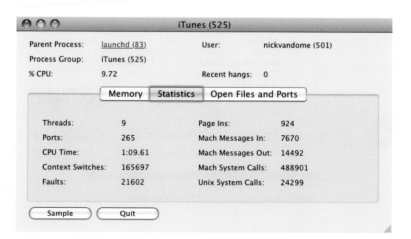

4 Double-click on a program to see its individual details

...cont'd

System Profiler

This can be used to view how the different hardware and software elements on your Mac are performing. To do this:

1 Open the Utilities folder and double-click on the System Profiler icon

System Profiler

2 Click on the Hardware link and click on an item of hardware

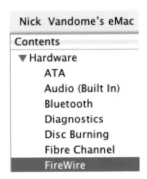

3 Details about the item of hardware, and its performance, are displayed

```
FireWire Bus:

  Maximum Speed:  Up to 400 Mb/sec

      iSight:

        Manufacturer:      Apple Computer, Inc.
        Model:             0x8
        GUID:              0xA270004082B59
        Maximum Speed:     Up to 400 Mb/sec
        Connection Speed:  Up to 200 Mb/sec
        Sub-units:
```

4 Click on software items to view their details

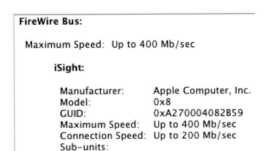

Dealing with crashes

Although Macs are rightly known for their stability, there are occasions when something goes wrong and a program crashes or freezes. This is usually denoted by a spinning colored ball (known as the Spinning Beach Ball of Death). Only rarely will you have to turn off your Mac and turn it on again to resolve the problem. Usually, Force Quit can be used to close down the affected program. To do this:

1. Once the spinning ball appears, click under the program's name on the Dock

2. Select Force Quit from the menu

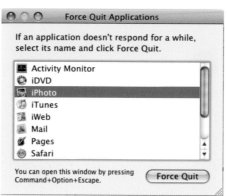

Application Not Responding

Keep in Dock
Open at Login
Show in Finder
Hide
Force Quit

or

Don't forget

It is unusual for Macs to freeze completely. However, if this does happen, hold down the start button for a few seconds until your Mac turns off. You should then be able to start it normally.

1. Hold down the Command (Apple), Alt and Esc keys at the same time

2. Click on the non-responding program

Force Quit Applications

If an application doesn't respond for a while, select its name and click Force Quit.

- Activity Monitor
- iDVD
- iPhoto
- iTunes
- iWeb
- Mail
- Pages
- Safari

You can open this window by pressing Command+Option+Escape.   Force Quit

3. Click on the Force Quit button  Force Quit

Backing up

Backing up data on your Mac is a chore, but it is an essential one: if the worst comes to the worst and all of your data is corrupted or lost then you will be very grateful that you went to the trouble of backing it up. Macs have a number of options for backing up data.

Burning discs

One of the most traditional methods of backing up data is to burn it onto a disc that can then be stored elsewhere. These days this is most frequently done on CDs or DVDs. To do this:

Don't forget

The CD/DVD burner on a Mac is known as a SuperDrive.

1 Insert the CD/DVD into the CD/DVD slot

2 Select for the disc to be shown in the Finder

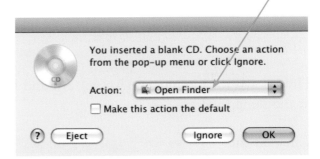

You inserted a blank CD. Choose an action from the pop-up menu or click Ignore.

Action: 🎵 Open Finder

☐ Make this action the default

(?) (Eject)   (Ignore) (OK)

Hot tip

If a CD or DVD does not burn successfully, try a different brand of discs. Sometimes the coating on some discs can cause a problem with the disc burner.

3 Locate the item you want to copy

Mac Seniors

4 Drag it onto the disc name in the Finder

5 Click on this icon to burn the disc

184

Time Machine

Time Machine is a Mac program that takes a lot of the pain out of backing up. To use Time Machine you have to have an external hard drive attached to your Mac, as this is where the backup is saved to. To use Time Machine:

1 Attach an external hard drive

2 Click on this icon on the Dock

3 Click on the Set Up Time Machine button

4 Click on the Choose Backup Disk button and select an external drive

Beware

If an external hard drive is not attached to your Mac you will not be able to use Time Machine and a warning message will appear when you try and set it up.

185

5 Drag this button to On

6 Click on the Time Machine icon on the Dock

Time Machine Preferences...
Back Up Now
Browse Other Time Machine disks...
Remove from Dock

Show Time Machine

7 Click on the Back Up Now link to starting backing up with Time Machine

...cont'd

Backup

Backup is a program that can be downloaded from .Mac and then used to back up files to your iDisk, so that they are saved in an online environment. To do this:

Don't forget

Backup can be downloaded from your .Mac account once you have logged in. Click on the Backup link on your homepage and follow the instructions.

186

1 Download Backup from your .Mac account

2 Click on the Backup icon on the Dock or access it in the Applications folder

3 Select to back up your files to your iDisk

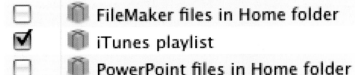

4 Check on the items you want included in the backup

☐ 📦 FileMaker files in Home folder
☑ 📦 iTunes playlist
☐ 📦 PowerPoint files in Home folder
☑ 📦 Word files in Home folder
☑ 📦 Files on Desktop
☑ 📁 Computer Step

5 Click on this button to add other items to the backup

6 Click on this button to select options for your backup to be performed automatically

7 Click on the Backup Now button to start the backup

Index

A

Accounts
  Household.
      See iWork: Household accounts
  Login options   162–163
  Multiple   160–161
ActiveShopper   122
Activity Monitor   180–181
Address bar.   *See* Websites: Address bar
Address book
  Compiling   46
  Creating a group   47
Airport   170
All-hotels   119
Ancestry   120
Apple
  History   8
Apple Menu   12
Applications folder   38
Aqua   10

B

Backgammon
  Online   130
Background
  Changing   14
Backing up   184–186
  Backup   186
  Burning discs   184
  Time Machine   185
Backup.   *See* Backing up: Backup
Banking
  Online   127
Bookmarks. *See also* Websites: Bookmarks
  Adding   111–112
  Bookmarks Bar   111
  Bookmarks Menu   112
Boot Camp   21
Boot Camp Assistant   21

Bridge
  Online   130
Browsers
  Setting a homepage   108

C

Calculator
  Using   96
Calendar
  Adding   48–50
  Adding more   49
  Mini Calendars   50
  To Do list   50
Camera
  Connecting   56
Carnival   119
CD/DVD slot   11
Chess
  Playing   84
Choice Hotels International   119
Color adjustments.
       See iPhoto: Color adjustments
Color display   16
Column view   26
Covers   28
Crashes
  Dealing with   183
Creating a photo album.
       See iPhoto: Photo albums: Creating
Cropping photos.   *See* iPhoto: Cropping
Cruises.com   119

D

Dashboard   88
Dictionary
  Accessing   87–88
  Applications   87
  Dashboard   88

Dock
  Adding and removing items   31
  Customizing   30
  Magnification   30
  Menus   31
  Overview   29
  Size   30
  Stacking items   32–33
Documents folder   45
Downloading photos.
     See iPhoto: Downloading photos
Drop Box.
     See Network: File sharing: Drop Box
DVD/CD slot   11

E

Earbuds   74
eBay   124–126
  Auctions   124
  Buying items   124–125
  Buy It Now   124
  Selling items   126
Effects.   *See* iPhoto: Effects: Adding
Email
  Account Information   132
  Attaching photos
    Attach button   136
    Photo Browser   137
  Creating   134–135
  Junk email   139
  Mailboxes
    Adding   133
  Setting up   132
  Stationery   138
Enhancing photos.
     See iPhoto: Enhancing photos
Ethernet   11
Expedia   118
Exposé   36

F

Familysearch   120
Family history
  Researching   120
Files
  Creating   42
  Saving   43
Finder   12
  Menu bars   12
  Overview   24
  Sidebar   25
  Viewing items   26
Finding things   52–54
  Using Finder   52
  Using Spotlight   53
Firewire ports   11
Folder structure
  Creating   45
Force Quit   183

G

Games
  Online   130
GarageBand   75–76
  Creating music   75
Genealogy   120
  Family tree
    Creating   121
Genealogy.com   120
Google   52, 110
Google Maps   129
Graphical User Interface   8
Groups
  Creating in .Mac   158
GUI.   *See* Graphical User Interface

H

Headphones 74
History.   *See* Websites: Browsing history
Homepage
    Setting 108
Home movie
    Sharing. *See* iDVD: Sharing a home movie
Hotels.com 119
Household expenses 86

I

IBM-compatible PCs 8
iCal 48–50
iCards
    Sending 156–157
iChat 140
Icons view 26
iDisk 144–146
    Creating 144
    Preferences 146
    Viewing online 145
iDVD 80–83
    Sharing a home movie 80–83
iLife 56, 58
iLink 11
iMac 8, 9
iMovie 78–79
    Home movie
        Creating 78–79
Internet
    Accessing 104
Internet Service Provider 104
iPhone 8
iPhoto 56, 58–67
    Color adjustments 64
    Cropping 63
    Downloading photos 58
    Effects
        Adding 66
    Enhancing photos 63–66

Photo albums
    Creating 61–62
    Removing red-eye 65
    Sharing photos 67
    Slideshows 60
    Viewing photos 59
iPod 8, 68
    Adding 73
ISP.   *See* Internet Service Provider
iTunes 8, 68–72
    Adding a playlist 70
    Downloading music 71–72
    Organizing music 69–70
    Playing music 68
    Radio
        Listening to 77
iTunes store 71
iWeb 152–155
iWork 86
    Budget 97
    Creating a letter 89–91
    Creating a presentation 100–102
    Formatting a newsletter 92–95
    Household accounts 97–99
    Keynote 100
    Numbers 97
    Pages 89

J

Jobs
    Steve 8
Joint Photographic Experts Group. *See* JPEG
JPEG 21

K

Keyboard
    Customizing 20
Keyboard shortcuts 20

L

Leopard	9, 10
Letters	
Creating	86.
See also iWork: Creating a letter	
Links.	*See* Websites: Links
List view	26
Login options. *See* Accounts: Login options	

M

Macintosh	
First	8
Macs	
Customizing	13
Desktops	9
Laptops	9
MacBook	9
MacBook Air	9
MacBook Pro	9
Mac Mini	9
Mac Pro	9
Turning on	12
Types	9
Mac desktop	12
Maps	
Online	129
Menu bar.	*See* Websites: Menu bar
Microsoft Office	21, 86
Microsoft Powerpoint	100
Microsoft Windows	8
Sharing with	21
Modem	11
Mouse	
Customizing	19
Multimap	129
Multiple users	
Adding users	160–161
Switching between	164

Music

Creating. *See* GarageBand: Creating music	
Downloading.	
See iTunes: Downloading music	

N

Navigation bars.	
See Websites: Navigation bars	
Network	
Creating	170–172
File sharing	173–176
Accessing other computers	174
Drop Box	176
Guest users	175
Setting up	173
Newsletters	
Formatting.	
See iWork: Formatting a newsletter	
Norton	178

O

Opening items	
From the Dock	44
In the Finder	44
Operating system 10.	*See also* Leopard
Organizing music.	
See iTunes: Organizing music	
OS X	8, 9

P

Parental controls	165–169
Content controls	167
Enabling	165
Log controls	169
Mail and iChat controls	168
System controls	166
Time controls	169

PDF   21
Photoshop Elements   58
Playing music.   *See* iTunes: Playing music
Playlists.   *See* iTunes: Adding a playlist
Portable Document Format.   *See* PDF
PowerBook   8
Presentations   86
   Creating.
     See iWork: Creating a presentation
   For clubs or charities   100
PriceGrabber   122
PriceRunner   122
Princess Cruises   119
Printers
   Adding   55
Print driver   55
Programs
   Installing   39
   Mac   38
   Opening   38

Q

Quartz   10
Quick Look   27

R

Radio
   Listening to. *See* iTunes: Radio: Listening to
RAM   181
Red-eye
   Removing. *See* iPhoto: Removing red-eye
Reminders   51
Removing items   40
Resolution
   Screen   16
Restarting   22
RootsWeb.com   120

S

Safari   105, 108
Screen burn   15
Screen saver
   Changing   15
Screen size
   Changing   16
Searching   52–54
   The Web   110
Search box.   *See* Websites: Search box
Security
   Overview   178
Sharing online
   With .Mac   142–143
Sharing photos. *See* iPhoto: Sharing photos
Sharing photos online.   *See* Web Gallery
Shopping
   Online   116–117
     Guidelines   116
Shutting down   22
Skype   140
Sleeping   22
Slideshows.   *See* iPhoto: Slideshows
SnapBack   114
Software
   Updating   179
Sophos   178
Spaces   34–35
Spinning Beach Ball of Death   183
Spotlight   52, 53–54
   Preferences   54
Stacks.   *See* Dock: Stacking items
Stickies   51
Stocks and shares
   Online   128
SuperDrive   184
Synchronizing
   With .Mac   147
System Preferences   13
   Show All   13
System Profiler   182

T

Tabs
  Using   109
Telephone calls   140
TextEdit   86
Text chatting. *See* iChat
Text size
  Changing   17
  Zoom   17
Time Machine. *See* Backing up: Time Machine
Toolbar.   *See* Websites: Toolbar
Trash   40
Travelocity   118
Tripadvisor   118

U

Uniform Resource Locator. *See* URL
Universal Access   17
Universal Serial Bus. *See* USB ports
UNIX   10
URL   108
USB ports   11

V

Vacation
  Booking   118–119
  Cruises   119
  Hotels   119
Video chatting. *See* iChat
Viewing files
  Without opening   27
Viewing photos. *See* iPhoto: Viewing photos
Volume
  Adjusting   18

W

Wayne
  Ronald   8
Web
  Overview   105–107
  Searching   110
Website
  Creating your own.   *See* iWeb
Websites
  Address bar   105
  Bookmarks   107
  Browsing history   113
  Links   107
  Main content   105
  Menu bar   106
  Navigation bars   106
  Price comparison 122–123
  Search box   106
  Tabs   107
  Toolbar   106
Web Gallery   148–150
  Viewing   151
Widgets   88
Windows
  Closing   37
  Enlarging   37
  Minimizing   37
  Working with   37
Windows Vista   21
Windows XP   21
Word processing   89
World Wide Web   104
Wozniak
  Steve   8

Z

Zoom in
  On text   17